Happy Neighborhood

Courtesy South Florida Libraries, Special Collections.

Happy Neighborhood

essays and poems

THOMAS HALLOCK

MERCER UNIVERSITY PRESS
Macon, Georgia

MUP/ P681

© 2023 by Mercer University Press
Published by Mercer University Press
1501 Mercer University Drive
Macon, Georgia 31207
All rights reserved

27 26 25 24 23   5 4 3 2 1

Books published by Mercer University Press are printed on acid-free paper
that meets the requirements of the American National Standard for
Information Sciences—Permanence of Paper for Printed Library Materials.

Printed and bound in the United States.

This book is set in Adobe Caslon Pro.

Cover/jacket design by Burt&Burt.

ISBN   978-0-88146-909-7

Cataloging-in-Publication Data is available from the Library of Congress

Contents

Yellow moon sets
at dawn, orbiting
heedless of us.

MERCER UNIVERSITY PRESS

Endowed by

TOM WATSON BROWN
and
THE WATSON-BROWN FOUNDATION, INC.

Introduction

Tree Fort

I never should have groused about a home blessing. But Julie brought this book, some guide to rituals and spells, that she dug out the day we moved in. I felt blindsided. I thought we already had a tradition. Whenever we moved into a new apartment or home, this our fourth, we would order takeout from a Chinese restaurant, sit on a mattress on the floor, eat from the containers, and drink white wine. But here she brought her own ritual. She wanted to sprinkle salt in the corner of each room, light a candle, and say what we hoped for that room. I didn't want to sprinkle salt. Or light candles. I wanted to drink. I never asked to move to Florida. So I picked a fight.

The year was 2002. Our house needed work, which was fine, because I needed a job. We moved here, to the Happy Neighborhood, with only Julie employed, and we could not afford much, so we bought this project. Old knob-and-tube wiring shot through the rafters. Galvanized steel plumbing rusted into the dirty sand. A stairway to the attic, where the old owners had hung grow lights for a bumper crop of weed, was not up to code. A leak along the chimney had rotted out the plaster above the hearth. I spent five years checking off chores from an endless list—stripping, scrubbing, hammering, patching, and painting my way home.

Popular myth holds that people move to Florida in search of paradise. Ponce de Leon, the legend goes, sought the Fountain of Youth. (Closer to the truth, slave hunting and political rivalries squeezed him out of Puerto Rico.) A job took me here, someone else's job, and I struggled with the move. Julie felt liberated from winter. I sweat through summer. She slid into tenure at her university. I cobbled together a career from scraps. I looked for ways to love this often dysfunctional state—I labored over our property, learned the plants, and paddled the rivers. Eventually I found my footing professionally. But my real guide to happiness was a dog, a barky hound named Virgil who led me through my middle years, "mezzo del cammin." It was a bad literary joke, the Latin poet Virgil being Dante's guide through the Inferno, but also the reference to an underrated poem by Henry Wadsworth Longfellow. Letting the years slip from me, I had been nurturing fruitless scholarly aspirations, fueled mostly by egotism, getting nowhere.

Up until the month he died, February 2018, Virgil and I would follow a ritual. I started most mornings with my crooked yoga poses, then Virgil and I would walk four blocks down to Tampa Bay. We would pause at a bench before sunrise at Lassing Park, a strip of grass mowed by the city. Virgil sniffed the bushes while I watched the horizon blink from indigo to a pinkish umber. I counted my breaths and, in a childish rage at the beauty before me, tried settling my thoughts.

One morning, we got back home, and while the dog napped I drafted this poem:

> By the end of February
> the browning oranges have
> hardened on their stems,
> and the morning light
> off the bay strikes
> the hearth windows
> at such an angle
> as if to create a forest
> in our living room.
> The heart pine glows.

I've revised this poem more times than I care to admit over the past fifteen years. (A final version appears on page 84.) The opening was clunky, so I stripped away excess words; because my lines can be

2

a tad grammatical, I shortened the sentences. I also pared down the conjunctions because someone told me that's what poems do.

So why all this effort?

Any poet will tell you that a writer needs tradition. Models, precedents, examples help make the poems work. In my case, the seventeenth century has served as a touchstone. I admire how someone like George Herbert prays in verse. Anne Bradstreet, likewise, rhymes her way to peace with Puritan Massachusetts. Here is Bradstreet in one of her most famous turns, on the burning of her house. One can imagine her mixed emotions, as flames scorched the timbers on a frigid New England night:

> And when I could no longer look
> I blest His name that gave and took,
> That laid my goods now in the dust;
> Yea, so it was, and so 'twas just—
> It was His own, it was not mine.
> Far be it that I should repine.

Bradstreet threads between sarcasm and resignation, alienation and return. *Far be it* that I should repine.

We can learn a lot from the devotional poets. Bradstreet, Herbert, and the rest provide clear instructions on how to find happiness where you live. For a group lumped together as the "Metaphysicals," theologically they don't offer much. Sure, they write about God and Jesus and Eternal Life, but I study them today to make peace with myself. The gaze towards Heaven always leads back home.

Domestic tranquility has never come easy to me. Paradise did not settle me in Florida; family did. After Julie and I bought our house in St. Petersburg, my sister and brother-in-law moved here too; their sons were born at the city hospital up the road. Next came my mother and after her a brother. Then Julie and I adopted a kid. Having a child here made me fully Floridian—both emotionally and bureaucratically.

Poems from the park helped me process these transitions.

Our son never asked to be adopted. After a honeymoon period, children who transition from foster care must unpack devastating trauma. The kids reject authority; they act out. From the street, our home could sound pretty ugly. (Neighbors called the cops on us more than once.) As my son worked through his rage, a pain no child could ever wrap words around, I doubled down on the search for happiness.

This should not at all sound trite; it was survival. Julie and I were left with only one option as parents—try to replace the bad memories with good. We were in triage. The kid and I built a tree fort. Then a skateboard ramp. We fished and camped. A friend gave him a kite, which hung on his bedroom wall until adolescence, when it got replaced by a Green Day poster. But the kite is still tucked into the back of his closet.

> …though sometimes I worry
> how you've grown accustomed
> to the steady pull of anger,
> to the tug of opposition which
> gives shape and lift to your days.

A walk to the bay, until Virgil died, would clear my head.

The morning ritual helped me figure out where I need to be as a parent. I tried, unsuccessfully, to imagine his wordless alienation:

> …no bruised resentment
> about his adoption,
> just heron tracks and
> the silhouettes of rays,
> bedded in the sand.

How do you build a bridge of empathy when the child wants no part of your words?

When a writing idea hits me, I make a file. I think in manila folders. One morning, as several scraps came together, I started a file called "Lassing Park." The title did not last long. That same afternoon, a chapbook by the state poet laureate (and neighbor) Peter Meinke came in the mail. His little collection was titled *Lassing Park*. So I changed the name of my file to "Happy Neighborhood," but I kept the idea for a book.

The project has purpose.

Happy. Not willfully ignorant or complacent. But content: the work of settling one's spirit, filling the hole in my heart that my wife says I project onto my kid. When Julie and I adopted a child, we adopted his adoption.

Poetry helps me sift through the secondhand grief. I think about George Herbert's collar, about his desire to flee from vague discontent. "I will abroad," he writes angrily. I think about Anne Bradstreet's restless, reassuring intelligence. I remember the core lessons of their poems—gratitude, letting go. Julie and I cannot dismiss a child's prior hurt. But we can at least give him a place to call his own.

Or maybe he has that already.

The kid and I built the tree fort with scrap lumber from a ten-year renovation. We framed the beams against a stand of cherry laurels, hung old lap siding and screen windows on two sides, and half a door to make a hinged wall over the neighbor's yard.

After we finished, the kid seemed to lose interest in the tree fort—or so I thought. He said there's nothing to do up there. But when I mentioned leaving Florida, setting sail against the ceaseless breeze of my own undefined restlessness, the kid wanted nothing of it. "We can never sell this house," he said. I asked him why.

The kid said, "My tree fort is here."

Part One

Fathers

Thomas Hallock

Poetry Time with Zackary, who was learning about metaphor in school

—for the teachers at James B. Sanderlin Elementary School

> "Write about how you're doing,"
> my son says to me.

Like how it feels when you
have discovered for yourself
how to construct a ramp from
scrap wood and cinder blocks,
and how it feels for me, a new
dad, to listen with one ear open
as you and your friends jam
pedals up and down the alley,
and how, even now, my own
body memory leans back in
sympathy to lift the handlebars
at the feather's crest of a ramp,
squatting off the seat, flying
in a shared exhilaration
greater than fear, defying
gravity in this short-lived
arc then landing the rear
tire back in the sand.

> "That's good," he says, "but can you put
> some chocolate milk in it?"

Okay! A whole tray of snacks,
pizza stuffers, whole milk
with two scoops of Ovaltine,
because homework is done

and the evening cradles
endless Autumn afternoons
like a wheeled eternity.
Time will slip a sprocket
for you soon enough, son.
Until then, after snacks,
you can walk your friends
home while I straighten up
and load the dishwasher
(for the third time today)
then I'll find some way to say
to an eleven-year-old, as
new father to new son, "yes
Zackary, I'm doing fine."

Thomas Hallock

After the Adoption, an impossible conversation

We could give it a shot.
We could try flying that
old blue and green kite,

the one shaped like a turtle's
back. Why not? It's hung in
your room two years now.

I even bought string, though
we would have to dig it up,
I forget where your mom put it,

I want to say in the cabinet
below the sink; and while
looking, I should also say,

I worry how you've grown
accustomed to this tug of
anger, how opposition gives

shape and lift to your days.
Now that I'm living backwards
I try to quiet my discontent—

It's not the same, I realize,
no child should ever ask,
"is this really my dad?"

But you won't always be
a child and the fighting
has to stop. There are fish

for us to catch, bikes to ride,
rage that needs articulation,
and kites for us to fly.

Square Grouper (or how certain policies of the Ronald Reagan administration entered into my home)

Square Grouper (noun, slang):
what fishermen, cops,
Coast Guard and stoners
call bales of Colombian cannabis
pressed into polyethylene bags
by kitchen trash compactors
and destined, perhaps,
for the derelict
docks off Salt Creek,
the polluted inlet
just north of this
happy neighborhood
where my family now lives.
Before the Coasties
could intercept drug
runners on the Gulf,
traffickers would toss
their cargo overboard,
leaving in their wake
tightly wrapped bales of
half-submerged marijuana.
Square grouper, joke was,
bobbing there on the open sea.
Those were simpler times,
before cocaine replaced cannabis
as Colombia's leading export,
and before the right-wing
Contras in Nicaragua expressed
a need for Kevlar, rifles, hand
grenades and land mines,
all those accoutrements necessary

to overthrow a freely elected
democratic government
in the western hemisphere;
so the Contras trafficked drugs
for the CIA, cocaine proving
to be the most fungible,
and which, when cut
with baking soda then
heated in a glass pipe,
releases a pure vapor
benzoylmethylecgonine
that when inhaled yields
a euphoric invincibility
like no other, lasting
ten minutes, at best.
It is the devil, I'm told,
a blowtorch scorching
neural receptors after just
a second or third dose, leaving
users longing for no other pleasure
except that of more cocaine,
which is, in fact, how we got our son,
whom sheriffs removed at four years old
from a filthy home with an empty
fridge, syringes on the floor,
his first question to the elderly
angel who picked him up being,
will my next house smell like poop?
It did not and I cannot express
what our society owes foster parents,
the guardians of in-between lives,
our son's biological mother failing
to appear in court, if not crack
then some other drug, caring
more for her next pill or hit
than the rambunctious child

she brought into this world,
then fast-forward four years
when the court ruled us a family,
partial product of an epidemic
our government introduced
to L.A. streets, justified by the
Communist menace in a country
most of us cannot place on a map,
funded by the covert export
from a second nation whose
name we cannot even spell,
with an "o," not a "u."
Spell it! C-O-L-O-M-B-I-A.
Because justice has a way
of turning back around.

Interlude

Happy Neighborhood
(or it's not that simple, Philip Larkin)

"Poetry's purpose is to teach other people and to touch their hearts," Ted Kooser intones. With a disarming earnestness, the former poet laureate explains that poems should "keep the obstacles" between author and reader "to a minimum." The word "purpose" looms large in Kooser's prescription.

So to my purpose.

We live in a time in which men have been inconvenienced to rethink who we are. *Who they are.* The implications are important, even dire. In order to pass forward love to our children, fathers must reconsider where we come from—what pain or proper paths we carry in our hearts, how we came to be. Poems help map this necessary search.

A "happy" person, of course, does not live clear of complications.

Happiness ≠ infantile gratification.

If anything, a long literary tradition of aggrandizing the male ego got in the way of my finishing poems. I grew up on textbooks and anthologies that equated aesthetic production with unrequited love. Or that treated gnomic imagery like some sort of intellectual kung fu match. I have noodled with poetry my entire adult life, and for years I succeeded mostly in torturing myself with half-finished attempts. Then a change occurred. I eased up on the masculinity bit. Poems started completing themselves. Maybe it's a perspective that comes with age.

Return to my core scenario. In 2001 Julie and I moved to St. Petersburg, Florida. The city is a subtropical paradise, founded on leisure. A Chamber of Commerce flyer from 1922 promised freedom from consumption, ennui, age, and strife. "Where all the time is Summer and to breathe is ecstasy!" the brochure promised. "Health, pleasure, youth and life find their greatest measure of expression." To this day, tourists flock to where we live, a vibrant downtown just twenty minutes from lovely gulf beaches. Who could ever feel unhappy in Florida?

Except that it was never my choice to live here.

When we relocated, I had no job, no prospect, no friends. The politics (and people) were (and are) crazed. To keep me busy through these transitional years, Julie and I bought the house in our happy neighborhood, just south of downtown. We found a classic St. Petersburg home. "Wide porches, numerous windows and doors," as boosters described, bringing "thorough ventilation and life out-of-doors." Built on a relic dune blocks off Tampa Bay and before air conditioning, the home matched in architectural features what the Chamber of Commerce described. A structure designed to take advantage of the physical elements—high ceilings, double-sashed windows, a generous front porch positioned to catch evening and morning breezes. A fireplace in the living room to cut the occasional chill of a Florida winter. And of course a dog.

Fast-forward another ten years, to 2010, when Julie and I became parents.

The house and happy neighborhood would be where we raised our one son, the little boy (now a young man) named Zackary. Julie and I could not have children the old-fashioned way, biologically, and neither of us ever had interest in changing diapers, so we adopted Zack out of foster care. Zack was eight years old at the time, burning more energy than even the usual third grader could control. He came to us with anxieties that were not of his own making, and to cope with those anxieties, he carried a virtual pharmacy in his backpack.

Little known, if unsurprising fact: When a child in "the system" experiences behavioral issues, the state reevaluates his or her mental health plan. That plan, even after monumental changes in the child's life (such as moving to a new foster home), cannot be altered without a court order. Florida State Statute 743.0645 defines "medical care and treatment" for children under the ward of the state as routine doctor and dentist visits, blood work, immunizations, but not the "provision of psychotropic medications."

Anyone who has ever sought serious mental health care grasps the problem immediately. Psychiatry works through trial and error—take this pill, see if it works; if not, or if harmful side effects appear, try another; and so on, down the list. Ritalin, Aderall, Abilify, etc. When a change of medication requires a court order, however, psychiatrists have no option but to raise dosage. Instead of finding the right medicine, welfare doctors overprescribe.

And so our eight-year-old son arrived to us with two asthma inhalers, over-the-counter allergy tablets, Ritalin three times a day (to help focus in school), sleeping pills (to come off the Ritalin), a pill to prevent bed wetting (because of the sleeping meds). All told, seven different medications. When I took Zack to a physician for the first time, I brought along his medication in a gallon-sized Ziploc bag. Concerned for the child, the doctor held up the bag of pills and scowled at me. As if this were my decision. Very few people grasp the challenges of adoption trauma. Least of all bougie pediatricians.

Medication alone would not solve this mess. Julie and I inherited an almost impossible task, one we barely understood ourselves, when we adopted out of foster care. Friends, family, and almost complete strangers saw the story as heartwarming. "He's so lucky to have you," we heard. There is a disconnect, largely upheld through naiveté and popular culture. *We should be happy.*

In the usual adoption story, Daddy Warbucks slowly warms to Little Orphan Annie. Act I of the adoption plot opens with a chorus of abandoned kids singing "It's a Hard Knock Life." In Act II the child meets an unsuspecting adult, one whose coffers are full but whose heart is empty. An internal conflict or misunderstanding ensues, teasing out the audience's emotions, then at some point, before or after intermission, the hardships melt away. We reach the final act with the curly red-headed white girl, safe in her new home, belting out a finale chorus of "Tomorrow."

Ditto, *Despicable Me*. Second verse, same as the first. A trio of orphaned girls stumble onto the home of genius arch-villain, Gru. Despite plans to take advantage of the loveable orphans, the villain's cold heart melts; his plans to rule the world are interrupted by the middle child's ballet recital. Gru adopts, of course, and the movie closes with the new family bonding over a revised bedtime story.

This happy ending, repeated again and again, creates unrealistic expectations for both parents and kids. In our adoption training, a county-sponsored course called Model Approaches to Positive Parenting (MAPP), we heard the contradicting stories. Social workers want children to heal, they want successful placements, and the emphasis in MAPP class falls on attachment. Make a "Life Book," the counselors suggested—a kind of craft-book story for the child that will bridge the chasm of trauma he or she must negotiate. Because they were also realists, with principles tested by field experience, the same social workers offered countering and far more realistic narratives than a Life Book.

In one very helpful demonstration, the MAPP leaders explained the psychology of a hurt child through the metaphor of a paper cup. To illustrate the child's trauma, a social worker cut a hole in the bottom of the cup. A second social worker then poured water into the torn cup, which of course leaked as fast as it could be filled. The rosy language of adoption-speak is that Julie and I would provide a "forever home" to the child in need; at the same time, the course leaders emphasized, we had been tasked with filling a cup that cannot be filled. That is the more accurate narrative for healing a wounded child.

Several poems in this little book come out of the painful process of adoption. As a new father, I was clueless about the emotional challenges before me. But as a literature professor, I had for myself at least a coping strategy that has served me throughout my adult life—writing.

A surprising amount of what we were going through is mere narratology. Wiser, more convincing psychologists warn us to avoid simple plot lines. A "story of adoption will continue to unfold with the telling and re-telling," Amal Treacher and Ilan Katz sagely observe. As we embrace more fluid concepts of identity, accepting a basic truth that one may never heal fully, we "allow others and ourselves the opportunity to re-interpret and feel events anew." The cup never fills entirely.

A "mature individual," Treacher and Katz remind us, lives with the contradictions and discontinuity. (We do the best we can at the time, my mom says, accepting past failures and forgiving our own imperfections.) With these poems, I find myself again drawn to one of my favorite periods of English literature, the seventeenth century. Authors who had experienced civil war, religious schisms, economic and political strife understandably felt as if the very dome of heaven had cracked; as their spiritual lives fractured, they turned to verse to inspect the damage. While seventeenth century (or Metaphysical) verse has been praised for its innovation and originality of imagery, I was unconsciously drawn to the process. Poetry serves as a mechanism, as spiritual-aesthetic device, for bending the wayward soul to the will of God. As to whether these pilgrim-poets ever found religious solace, I can't say, but the writers produced some pretty remarkable verse.

This process leads me back to fathers and sons. Not so much to God the Father (although I do have uses for traditional religion) as to my own dad. Parents in contemporary literature serve as easy piñatas. One of the maxims learned in a creative writing class is that any author who has survived high school possesses a lifetime of material to write about; over the past hundred years especially, parents take a beating. As Philip Larkin memorably wrote in his 1971 signature poem, "This Be the Verse":

They fuck you up, your mum and dad.
They may not mean to but they do.

Damning lines for sure, and for many, quite true.

But how to follow this opening? Larkin's short poem, just three stanzas, closes with a less-than-adequate solution:

Man hands on misery to man.
  It deepens like a coastal shelf.
Get out as early as you can,
  And don't have any kids yourself.

Every parent "hands on" their issues to children. The problems persist. We carry inherited childhood wounds into adulthood. That is a universal truth. My father's father died after a bender, scarring my own dad at an impressionable age, and so in ways that I am still unpacking, my own psychic makeup has been shaped by a grandfather whom I have never even met. And I would call my mom emotionally well balanced, but even into her eighties she still hears her mother's withering judgment.

But don't have kids? What do I do with that advice, especially after Julie and I have already adopted? The end-rhymes in "This Be the Verse" land so hard that I can almost forget how my own parents actually did a pretty good job. They loved me. What is the angst-ridden author to do?

So to my predicament: to push past Larkin's clear-eyed, though ultimately useless advice. The poems here started from a period before having a child, from around 2001, when Julie and I moved to our house. Born under a storm cloud, like the self-pitying chump in a newspaper comic strip, I turned to poetry in a conscious effort to find happiness. The writing fits within a broader spiritual practice: meditation, some rusty yoga, walking the dog to the park, deep breaths...*compose.*

The plot thickens, of course, with adoption.

If my job as a parent is to fill the paper cup with no bottom, replacing bad memories with good, how do I keep my own spirits up? Despite my private rain cloud, I focus on the reasons to be cheerful—I have a beautiful home, an affectionate spouse, and the security that comes from being white and middle class and in good health; I have employment that is also a creative outlet; my son possesses a beautiful soul and he continues to grow.

The disciplined pursuit of happiness (or good luck) can zap away mildewed negativity. But that is not to say my family's story has ever been easy. There is no happy ending. The premise of an adoption narrative tears easily, leaving gaping holes, and often, we feel afraid.

I may need a bigger Life Book.

Prayer for the Gulf, a bedtime story

When the little boy drummed, the buzzards circled, the ancestors noticed, and the flowers returned. Thousands upon thousands of rusty-winged fritillaries found the little boy, each holding a single palm filament in their crabbed front legs. The butterflies wove these filaments into a basket and carried the little boy away. The little boy kept drumming and the earth called back in full fluorescence. He drummed past the shopping mall, where spartina cracked open the concrete sidewalks, oysters whistled like jubilant fountains, the sea grass waved in approval, mangrove prop roots split the dimpled asphalt, the sumpish water ran clean again. Life returned to the bay. Red snapper teemed in the blue-green flats, manatees noshed along the collapsed seawalls, even the hammerheads were happy. The little boy kept drumming, but as the butterflies carried him further out to sea, his basket lost altitude. They had no nectar to fuel their flight. The little boy started to fall—he fell ten, twenty, a hundred feet, he almost crashed, but the little boy never lost faith, he kept drumming, and just before he struck water, four bald eagles caught the basket and carried him home, where his mom and dad were waiting, and the little boy fell fast asleep, safe and at peace, nested, with this somnolent prayer for the gulf.

Thomas Hallock

Naturalist's Elegy

—for Bill Belleville (1945–2020)

I dreamt about a ray last night,
or maybe it dreamt me
after it had been released
from the fossil Miocene.

Shards of tail bubbled through a spring
we were exploring with my son—
a boy beside the relic dune,
sifting through the sand—

A shark's tooth here, petrified wood,
this striated chip of bone—
he threw the tooth back in the spring
but took the ray's tail home.

Bill and I said our goodbyes—
Men often struggle finding friends.
Dirt road led to interstate—
Homework, dinner, bath, and then

On Sunday night, I dreamt this ray
or maybe it dreamt me—
tangled in a buoy off
a grass flat in the bay,

We yanked the line, we tugged and cursed,
and then the ray broke free—
the silent buoy floated back in place
and the ray swam out to sea.

Allegory, when someone called the cops

On the night my son shoved me, the hurt burned a hole in my heart so deep that it is visible from outer space—a narrow beam of light now escapes through the hole, this thin shaft of light is so bright that even at home we must talk around it, we duck and dodge mid-conversation while crossing the kitchen, the light won't shut off, no matter how hard I try, it follows me, swooshing across the counter-tops like a cat's bladed tail, capable of severing a limb. When I reach into the pantry for a box of cereal, or open the fridge for a carton of milk, the light is still there. Does it ever go dark? I cannot claim this damage as irreparable, though I do know how others have noticed something deeply and profoundly wrong. What parental gaffe defines this home? The light wrecks lives, it hampers the path of sat-ellites, cell phone calls drop, Super Bowl coverage momentarily stopped, the halftime show was ruined, the kid must live somewhere else—all because of this hateful beam, not sparked though kept alive by my own vestigial hurt, it's ridiculous, pathetic, a confrontation mine alone to process. I did not cause the tear in my heart from which the light escapes but it falls upon a father to forgive; my task is to heal. Don't ever tell me this is easy or fair.

Thomas Hallock

Interlude

Stapler Poem (or thanks for nothing, Ezra Pound)

"and they have lifted the new person free of the act...."
—*Sharon Olds, "The Language of the Brag"*

I.

Adopt a child and lives change. On the night Julie and I picked up Zack at the foster home, we stopped at Walmart for a flat screen TV. Three weeks later, I was driving an SUV.

We got a therapist and counseling became a twice monthly fixture on the family calendar. Most of the therapy was a waste, a string of futile strategies—cognitive behavior, play therapy, particularly misguided psychoanalysis, aimed to root out the rage of a nine-year-old who was more interested in Matchbox cars than self-reflection.

One counselor ordered my son to write lines for breaking house rules. Zack was to pen "I will not curse" or "I will not throw corn muffins into the ceiling fan" 20, 50, 100 times. Julie and I doubted the worth of the exercise but we did not want to undermine the therapist, so we played along.

Then I snuck in an alternative. Since Zack was studying poetry at school, we asked him to write creatively. It seemed like a more positive reinforcement—rather than scribbling out his punishment like a caricatured Bart Simpson.

Props to the kid's third grade teacher, Ms. Soule, for teaching him metaphor. Without picking up any handbook, not a single volume from his parents' overstuffed poetry shelf, the kid turned out this nifty extended simile:

> The best part of my day
> was when the three *chunk*
> of a family went

cluchunk and came together
like three papers and
a stapler, putting these
three members of
a family together.

About that opening line, some context. Before testosterone kicked the boy up to teenager, Julie and I closed each day with "the ritual." This ritual involved several steps—deep breaths, giving thanks, counting our blessings, sharing the best part of our day, and of course, a story. *When the little boy drummed, the buzzards circled, the ancestors noticed, and the flowers returned....*

The parents of adoptive children have no choice but to try replacing the bad memories with good. My mom helped me see this point; she always reminds me to focus on the positive.

I have learned a lot since adopting a child. Fatherhood has led me to understand the value of forgiveness, letting go, surrendering one's self to optimism and love. Because, really, what other option does the parent have?

With that emotional work in mind, I wrote my own stapler poem. Though I must concede, the kid has done a better job.

Kluchunk! With the punch
of a stapler, some bureau-
cratic angel notarizes
your new name:

Zackary Leroy Johnson
Armstrong-Hallock.

We have the papers
to prove it. Signed,
sealed, witnessed,
documented with
pictures, showing

we are a family.
So let it be, filed
in God's triplicate:
That I am your father
and she is your mom,
the past is not finished
but we three are one.

II.

The writing in *Happy Neighborhood* meditates on family and togetherness. I have tinkered with love poetry for my entire adult life; for years, I had gotten nowhere. Most of the time, I did not even get laid. On both counts, with failed productivity and lack of sex, I blame the aesthetics of estrangement.

Let's face it. Literary history honors the dysfunctional. You cannot sink a shovel into the long trench of English verse without digging up some author bent on opposition and resistance. The *Norton Anthology of English Literature*—Volumes A, B, C—presents scores of broken-hearted men but only a handful of successful fathers. Without formally surveying the entire canon myself, I'd wager a 10:1 ratio of disaffected guys to connected dads.

Take Ezra Pound, who describes his craft in the *ABC of Reading* like a bullying Bronx boxing coach. Pound's handbook opens with a "longish dull stretch" that the "student will have to endure." A "harsh treatment" awaits authors for whom Pound has no use. Only "the weak-hearted reader" will skim past the rigorous exercises. Pound answers only to the call of "vigorous-living men" (except Sappho, Pound really likes Sappho).

Having been reared academically on such dogmatism, if in barely less extreme form, I was not suited to consider writing on family terms. The old shibboleths—the trope of unrequited love, dysfunctional relationships—catered to my fruitless anger. Pound: "an old bitch gone in the teeth." Eliot and the women "talking of

Michelangelo" with his terrified Prufrock. Even the apologies, for modernist poets, come off as insincere. As a foregone conclusion:

> Forgive me
> they were delicious
> so sweet
> and so cold

Because this misogyny is so deep-seated, I accepted it as part of the literary landscape. Only when I started looking to poems that served my ends as a partner and dad did I actually finish something myself.

But that still leaves the question: is my work now any good?

III.

Before we adopted Zackary, Julie talked over her own childhood traumas with a counselor. The therapist asked Julie to write down hurtful memories. Julie journaled about getting a baseball, bat, and glove for her birthday. Her mother was a single mom; after someone gave Julie the bat and ball, she tried playing alone. It is the saddest childhood story I have ever heard. Julie would throw the ball, walk across the yard, throw the ball back, and retrieve it. Her game of catch did not last long.

To this day, Julie cannot catch anything—not a ball, not car keys. She wonders about her biological father, who is still alive and who left her as a baby. If I toss Julie something, with even the gentlest of warnings, she panics. I wrote this poem for Julie shortly after one of her therapy sessions.

> The gift did not matter much at all
> if there was no one else home,
> no one else to catch the ball.
>
> The therapist asked you to write it down,

to recall what it was like to grow up alone;
you said the gift did not matter much at all.

But is that not the point? When you get
the glove and bat and ball, you still need
someone to show you how to catch and throw.

The therapist asked again, is that everything you saw?
What else do you know from this story?
And you cried, the story did not matter,

You have dealt with it since you were small,
overcoming it all, no choice, on your own,
with no one else there to catch the ball.

When Julie turned forty, I took her to the driveway of our first
home. I showed her how to throw and catch a baseball. Early in our
relationship I took her to the ballpark and showed her how to keep
score. She took to the system immediately, even inventing her own
codes. (A cross for the sacrifice bunt.) If we are patient, we can heal
past hurt.

IV.

When Zack moved in, he and I played sports together. Basketball
was one of the few things we could do without fighting.

So I wrote this one, "The Genius of Basketball," on Valentine's
Day 2013. Zack kept the poem thumbtacked on his wall, until we
repainted his bedroom. I struggled with this poem for years, never
quite getting the rhyme scheme right. (It used to be four four-line
stanzas. Someday I'll probably change it back.) Here it is for now:

The genius of basketball
is how a simple ridged sphere
cups the inside of a player's palm,

so the ball is never that far away;
whether it bounces off a backyard
concrete slab, the endless hardwood
hope of Madison Square Garden
or an improvised dirt court on
some random Mongolian steppe,
the basketball always comes back—
you fly forward with a friend
on a give and go, running end
to end for the fast break,
flying past the last defender,
and with a spontaneity you
practiced since last December,
with a perfectly timed pass,
layup, two points, off the glass.

V.

What makes good writing? There are well-crafted poems and there are heartfelt poems, the kind of poems one hears at a public wedding anniversary or open mic. All poetry has its place.

As an English professor and a dad, I wonder about the tension between artistry and the work that writing actually does in our lives. Pound proclaimed that we should regard a poem "in terms of its own genius." As for the story behind it? Ezra Pound says, *posh.* "You can spot the bad critic when he starts by discussing the poet and not the poem."

The insistence on the object of art, apart from its creator, continues into the present-day conversation. "Poetry is a lot more important than poets," Ted Kooser concludes. One thing I have learned from teaching in English departments is that creative writing students rarely want to dial back the literary clock. (If students do turn back the clock, their sense of time is digital; for them, "old" poems mean written when clocks had hands.) Contemporary tastes, even processes, grew out of modernism and the work remains cast in a modernist mold.

Creative writing students famously refuse to be bribed, cajoled, even paid to take more than a single course from a period before 1900. (Except maybe Shakespeare—but *whatever.*) Kooser's *Poetry Home Repair Manual*, a representative guide, makes no apology for including only present-day voices. Is it any wonder that MFA chapbooks all have the same patina?

What then to say about the critic who insists on foregrounding the life behind his own process? How do we evaluate our own attempts? Do I get an "A" for effort? On my annual report for my job as English professor, I itemize my achievements for the previous year. The more we publish, or the greater the prestige of the journal where our writing appears, the higher the reward. The result is an academic industry that turns out more than its share of exquisitely constructed, less-than-meaningful verse, placed in the top echelon of literary journals and magazines. But a poem tacked onto the kid's bedroom wall—where friends could see? That, for me, is a well-placed publication. That is my brag. Top that, Ezra Pound, you fascist fuck.

Yesterday's Tomorrows, an insomnia poem

As the house shuts up, come May, we fasten down
the windows and dial the thermostat to a dry-ice chill

so our son can sleep and I make the still more foolish mistake
of checking email in my underwear, an act that should be illegal

in and of itself, and which leaves me vulnerable to
the raw paranoia that splinters any chance of rest,

nor is any match for Julie's post-menopausal bobcat,
her nightly ritual of pulling the comforter up to her chin

because the house is too cold then kicking our fitted top
sheet to the foot of the bed, causing me to snap awake

in a shivering sweat, my legs tangled in the comforter,
thoughts still stewing on that intestinal last email.

Sleep now impossible, I retreat to my hammock
on the front porch, where, cocooned in a blanket

and suspended in the grace of a breeze particular
to a state surrounded by water on three sides,

I let the heavy balm of Florida's midnight air
smooth away the fruitless machinations about

a job that consumes too much, that pays to spin
the tin fan around the electric compressor

to cool our home on an already cool night.
I count my blessings, especially for the son

who must quiet his hard-earned rage and who
needs to dream more than his insomniac dad.

Consciousness drifts in and out. Around three a.m.
a pre-summer rain falls, the horny invasive frogs

drown out the a/c, then a transfigured sky
clears into almost imperceptible dawn,

backlighting the shadow of a live oak to the east,
and before one last bout of desperation sleep

my unmedicated son awakes to pluck the hooked
hammock strings like a drug-addled Jimmy Page.

Julie would let me stay in but there is coffee
on the kitchen table already and I want to be

the father who carpools his child to school,
so I unfold from my hammock and rise

to face the morning, happy, exhausted,
forgetting yesterday's tomorrow today.

Shiners

—*after Peter Meinke,* The Shape of Poetry

I fish,
he catches bait.
Darkness pools
around us.

He catches bait.
Bedded rays
surround us.
"Ten minutes."

It's past bedtime
for the boy.
Ten minutes pass,
he asks again.

When you are ten
there is no time,
he asks again,
"One more cast."

There is no time.
Sun. Fish.
"One more cast...
Use this bait."

I fish,
he catches bait.
Darkness pools
around us.

Part Two

Sons

After *Adaptation*

"What if the writer is attempting to create a story where nothing much happens, where people don't change, they don't have any epiphanies, they struggle and are frustrated and nothing is resolved? More a reflection of the real world."
　　　　　　　　　　　　—*Charlie Kaufman, from* Adaptation

Don't tell me there's no story,
it's the ending we want,
the intensification. If a flower
is to bloom, like razed copper
reconfigured by the craftsman's hand,
we want its cousin, digitized,
in measureless time-lapse frames.

Stripping a Cabinet

I.

I keep my winter clothes in an old broom closet. The cabinet is free-standing and tall but not very deep. It is too narrow for a curtain rod, but I can bunch heavy coats across the top and let my sneakers, boots, and shoes pile up on the bottom. It is the kind of furniture that one keeps for its age and form, the kind that has outlived its original function but one hangs on to anyway. It is old, cheaply made to begin with, loved, and tied to the past with style. It has the original hardware; a steel plate over the door marks in retro script where it came from: "R.H. Macy & Company, Inc., 34th St. & Broadway—New York." I grew up with the cabinet, as did my dad, and so the piece represents a line of family history that we just barely share.

II.

In 1940, my father's father suffered a heart attack that widowed my grandmother at twenty-eight. She had one year of college at Smith, enough to dignify her but not enough to draw out a living, so she moved to an uncle's place near Great Neck, Long Island, where she raised three children. Nana was a tough but gracious, Depression-era lady: not taller than five feet, she had impeccable manners and a Canadian Club on the rocks each evening. She kept a cold faith in the stock market and Republican politics through the better part of a century. In 1973 she retired to Longboat Key, off Sarasota, where she surrounded herself with antique furniture, shells, crystal ashtrays, china, and photographs of the grandchildren. (Frozen under glass, the kids would stay on their best behavior.) Nana deserved quiet; she wanted a house to make perfect. She died of liver cancer in 1985. Her move to Florida, however, brought me that strange heirloom—the broom closet.

When his mother left Long Island, Dad unbolted the cabinet from the pantry and seized it like a relic. Nana cut family ties by moving to Florida, leaving our connections to be made primarily through furniture. My grandmother and I were never close; we saw her mostly on holidays. Every birthday, a check for ten dollars written out to Master Thomas Hallock came in the mail. The money went straight into the bank. The broom closet, meanwhile, held my best memories of childhood. We used it to store the stuff that no one had the heart to throw away: tangled fishing reels, my first baseball mitt, a croquet set, badminton rackets, deflated footballs, two wicker jai-alai gloves, a Frisbee that once belonged to the dog.

I grew up with the sports cabinet. It sat in our basement for years. The door warped shut, the inside mildewed, the plate on front rusted over, the foundation softened from dry rot. The closet became something we could not leave, and when my parents moved to their next home, in Connecticut, I took it with me.

Dad was delighted. He felt deeply for inanimate objects, family things especially. He insisted that I repaint the cabinet, inside and out, and for reasons I could not articulate, I agreed to do the job right. So two Saturdays after Thanksgiving, I set my heirloom on a pair of sawhorses and stripped the piece to its foundation. I pried off the Macy's tag, unscrewed the art-deco hinges and catch from the front, and dropped the fixtures into a bowl of turpentine. The door popped off its base; I reset the joints in a vise and glued the frame. While the glue dried, I slathered Strypeeze on one side. The top coat blistered open. Thirty years of use bubbled under the surface. I snapped on a pair of kitchen gloves, ran a putty knife over the hot paste, and watched the closet's different lives melt away. At the end of each stroke, I slapped the past from my putty knife into a coffee can—a toxic soup of turpentine, pink emulsion, and lead. The solution made the surface even more spongy. The wood had lost its resiliency; the cabinet gouged easily. I wiped the sweat from my face, and my forehead burned.

Halfway stripped, the surface was a mottle, a flat history that somehow defied the burying passage of time. Old uses of the piece met on a single, ahistorical layer: an ugly medley of yellow, green, and flat blue. Little islands of a lost narrative may have been revealed. My ventilation was not good, and my head spun from the turpentine and stripper.

My arms fell into an unconscious rhythm of scraping. Patches of green stuck to the sides and in the corners, collecting in a soggy pool mixed with blue flecks. I scraped a little harder at the edges. Dad never talked about his childhood much, not unless he had some lesson that he wished to impart. I can scarcely reconstruct his life before Great Neck, partly because the story never seemed straight. He clung to idyllic memories of a loving father, astute in business, on the verge of a financial breakthrough. Then death.

My aunt reminded me that their father was an alcoholic. Dad's dad would disappear on benders, leaving family and work for days, as he drank his way from Battery Park to the 21 Club in midtown Manhattan, then back home on the bar car of the Long Island Railroad. It was one Sunday morning after a long drunk when he sent my father to fetch the paper. Dad waited, or so he said; he rode his bike or pet the dog or fed the duck or did whatever it is that kids do when given a job by their parents. When he came back to the kitchen, his father's face had turned the color of a bruise. The doctor said my grandfather was dead before he hit the floor.

Victorian reserve stunted my father's recovery. We have never been a tribe of crepe-hangers. To this day, my family marks death with a cocktail reception or a memorial service—always restrained and sometimes months after the fact. This funeral was an exception: immediate and open casket. But adults only.

Dad told me the story only once, when I was in high school, after the father of one of my closest classmates had died. Dad said that after watching his father collapse to the floor, he needed to see a face; he needed an image that could replace the pooly memory of blood welling at the temples. His Aunt Bea and Uncle June wanted to help; they shielded Dad from the sight of a cadaver. My dad said that if he had hurried back to the kitchen, he could have called someone. He carried around this childhood guilt.

The loss healed poorly. Time scarred over the initial trauma, and a self-formed around (rather than from) an incomplete mourning, so that even now my grandfather remains among the living. This may not be unusual; still, I grew up near a pain that never cut. Dad could be aloof and easily wounded. He threw around powerful—but clumsy—emotions. Without ever realizing it, my brothers and I learned to negotiate with the stopped heart of a grandfather whom we had never met. The work of restoration erases distance. Stripping a cabinet closes time.

III.

I put away the putty knife. My temples throb slightly and the wood feels rotten. With a wire brush I can scratch off the last crumbs of melted paint. The next weekend, I will complete the job and recover what should have remained secret. I need to sand the surface, edge the corners, and smooth over the spot where some yellow still clings to the poplar grain. After a coat of primer, the enamel paint should take nicely. I can gloss over the gouges. But I would never have known the cabinet's history without first stripping away the dull blue, then the green and the ivory of previous generations.

My waspish family specializes in secrecy, and from those silences spring new stories. For years, I believed the job explained my father's fixation with furniture—wood speaks, I reasoned, when the family will not. Now I'm not so sure; I was never sure with him. Did Dad tell the story of his own father's death to communicate grief with me? Or to one-up my high school friend? To trump my teenage trauma? Even in silence, my father silenced others. His favorite tactic was speaking quietly to control a conversation. His voice always had to be the loudest in the room.

Requisite Poem from the Point of View
of a Kitchen Table

> *"It doesn't matter which leg of your table you make first, so long as the*
> *table has four legs and will stand up when you have finished it."* —
> *Ezra Pound,* ABC of Reading

Before I offer one word of advice,
first you must replenish me—
rub linseed mixed with lemon
deep into my grain to hide
the blanched ring left by
your careless mug of coffee
or the stain of curdled milk
that splashed without dignity
off yesterday's cereal bowl.
Refurbish me, condition me,
then, maybe, we can talk.

Because it's been a hard ten years
and you have thought too little
about the patience with which
I have born your morning papers,
past-due reminders, unsent mail,
and apologies to one another.

You could also stand to tighten
the slot screws at my corners.
My joints have grown weak.
I have carried your burden silently,
since you asked, because that is
what furniture does. Each morning
renews the hopes of a new day,
breakfast followed by lunch
and dinner, the child growing

Thomas Hallock

by inches then feet as the years
calcify into decades, until
you can barely shut the door
to your closets because they
overflow with unused stuff.

Your hearing loss worsens.

You will find I grow more stable
if you rub in oil on both sides;
the restored finish will also hide
the nicks of old arguments.

I ask only for this basic care
so the cycle may repeat itself:
when your future participled son
who has become his own man,
with his partner or spouse,
brood forthcoming, maybe not,
no difference…he will need
a well-constructed kitchen table,
at which point he will untwist
my spindled legs, counterclockwise,
so I can fit out the front door,
and carry me down the steps,
while you implore him,
"be careful with the joints,
when you tighten the slotted
screws try not to strip them,"
advice the boy (now a man)
rightly ignores, for he heard
these lectures decades ago,
and he will gently ladle me
onto a truck or van, cover me
with a quilted blanket or retired
bedspread (showing this care

because he claims me now)
and with a silent nod or
short wave that bypasses
all expectation…your
son will drive away.

My Mother Says

My mother says "a wasted life" about
anyone who disappoints her expectations.

She stayed with my father over a decade,
even after she knew about his affair.

My mother will live with secrets, holding on
to business she considers entirely her own.

My mother says that I should write whatever
I think is true, and for that I am grateful.

"Have I told you this story already,"
my mother asks, then she tells me again.

"Are you listening to me," she repeats,
knowing we have heard the story before.

My mother hears criticism from her own mother,
my grandmother, who has been dead for sixty years—

which is to say they really do fuck you up,
we tread slowly down this continental shelf.

My mother says, "don't let your
yesterdays ruin your tomorrows,"

and that she finally left my dad after her
therapist said, "Peter will never change."

My mother says that *Hamilton* changed
what is possible in musical theater.

She says she saw *Oklahoma* on Broadway—
but wait, that cannot be right, those dates

do not line up, though she has
seen some amazing theater.

My mother says that I should
try meditation.

She says Clark Gable was so handsome;
she loved his pencil-thin moustache.

My mother will take in a grown man who has been
reduced to fetal helplessness by mental illness.

My mother was an excellent nurse.
She says I should soak my swollen toe.

My mother says, "hello handsome," though
not to me; she says that to my older brother.

My mother drinks wine when she visits
then drives herself home. We worry.

My mother ventured out through
the pandemic—carefully, but still.

My mother just turned eighty-four.
She is not afraid of death, just senility.

My mother says she has led
a very fortunate life. She has.

Interlude

Short Observation on Andrew Marvell

The most emotionally unhealthy people I have ever met come out of PhD programs in English. It's a paradox. Where literature and writing should open a path, help clear a voice, the academy deepens insecurities. It blocks.

I will never forget the first time in graduate school that I summoned the nerve to ask a question. I had just enrolled part-time at NYU and I took a summer course, "The Age of Milton." We had read Andrew Marvell that week, and in class the teacher drew our attention to a conceit about parallel lines in Marvell's "Definition of Love." The Marvell is a poem in conversation with another poem. The week before, we had read John Donne's "A Valediction: Forbidding Mourning"—the more famous one, in which Donne likens love to the points of a navigational compass. Although the point of one compass "in the center sit," as the beloved roams, the other's soul "leans and hearkens after it." Even though the compass points spread apart, conjoined, they return to a pivot—such is love.

Marvell, I noticed, played with a similar conceit:

As lines, so loves oblique may well
Themselves in every angle greet;
But ours so truly parallel,
Though infinite, can never meet.

In class, a light bulb went off in my head. I raised my hand, eager to share.

It was a warm evening in Greenwich Village. Outside the open windows of our building, the old Triangle Shirt factory, traffic rattled in with the breeze. I held my hand high. A single bead of sweat trickled down my armpit, past my ribcage, almost to my belly. Ignoring the sweat, eager but terrified, I waited for acknowledgment. Finally, the professor called on me—a first-semester student, speaking for the first time. As soon as the words came out of my mouth, a fire truck stormed down the street. Because of the blaring siren, nobody heard my question. The professor asked me to repeat. I was mortified. I noted how Marvell's lines, "so truly parallel," parody the compass metaphor in Donne. The association sounded right in my head. Once in the space of classroom discussion, however, the same thought seemed forced. The observation felt almost trivial.

And it's true, I was missing the point. Through most of my graduate education, I focused on the externalities. A history of tricks and ideas, twists and tropes in the Great Tradition, which I was expected to absorb. Outside knowledge, without substance. Even though I am decades past grad school, both Julie and I still struggle to make sense of what we learned.

I am now twice the age I was then. To reacquaint myself with how I read twenty-five years ago, I recently pulled down a text from that class: *George Herbert and the Seventeenth-Century Religious Poets*. (Though we cull our library periodically, Julie and I never get rid of poetry.) The book was a Norton Critical Edition, standard at the time, with low production value and a monotone cover—just a basic, black and white sketch of Salisbury Cathedral on front. The volume had two parts. Part One was poems, Part Two selected scholarship. The purpose was to help young English majors (or grad students) read like junior professors.

My instructor, Anthony Low, wrote the lead essay for the second part. I didn't realize then, but it was kind of a big deal. Known among the grad students for his trenchant indifference to new turns in humanities scholarship, Low also happened to be a very good reader of devotional verse. His introductory essay, "Metaphysical and Devotional Poets," situated the texts in a seventeenth-century cultural and historical context. He explained the intersections of writing and religion during a bloody period for England. In one of the summary moments, Low made a requisite nod to T. S. Eliot,

who changed how critics would read "Metaphysical" poets through
the twentieth century. I recognized Eliot's famous name. (He wrote
Cats!) In the margins of my textbook, I dutifully underlined Low's
quote of a quote—a historically important tagline about the "dissociation of sensibility," or the use of unexpected images to describe
religious experience. Later, with the same blunt half-comprehen-
sion, I marked a sentence that explained where poets mined their
images: from "emblem books, religious iconography, illustrated Bi-
bles, stained-glass windows, and continental literature."

It was all surface stuff.

Throughout graduate school, I focused on the materialities of a
literary house. I wanted the blueprint (mainstream tradition, identi-
fied by Eliot) and the individual bricks (where authors got their images). But my readerly house was no home. Coming back to my old
textbook, years later, I see that I missed the point of Low's essay—
which actually holds up, and which explains how and why these poems worked in their time. Metaphysical poets dramatized a process,
the "inner movements of thoughts and feelings." These on-the-page
performances of religious crises can be "easy to ridicule," Low con-
cedes, but also capture compelling acts of affective-spiritual tuning.

The most memorable poems dramatize the path of a wayward
soul, who comes back to God after a crisis. England was being torn
apart. George Herbert's "The Collar" dramatizes the doubts of a
parish priest who longs to unyoke himself of his religious garment,
his obligations, his low-visibility clerical duties at a country church
outside Salisbury. The poem opens mightily:

I struck the board, and cried, "No more;
I will abroad!
What? shall I ever sigh and pine?
My lines and life are free, free as the road,
Loose as the wind, as large as store.

Anyone can identify the sentiment. The impatience with one's
lot in life, followed by a resolution to hit the open road. With an

admittedly awful pun (striking the communion table, the "board" or "pine"), Herbert proclaims his frustration. He vows to fly off: "Away! take heed; / I will abroad." In the midst of his ravings, however, God's voice returns. The Holy Parent calls back a prodigal son:

> But as I raved and grew more fierce and wild
> At every word,
> Methought I heard one calling, *Child*!
> And I replied *My Lord*.

This spiritual drama is either compelling or melodramatic, depending on where you are in life. Graduate students at NYU would not openly declare their affection for George Herbert. What use did we have for these religious performances? It was okay even to snicker. One read him privately.

Herbert challenges pretentions. The Norton Critical Edition included a revealing snippet from Samuel Taylor Coleridge (a poet, of course, but as PhDs know also an exceptionally astute critic). With disarming sincerity, Coleridge writes, "I find more substantial comfort, now, in pious George Herbert's 'Temple,' which I used to read to amuse myself with his quaintness—in short, only to laugh at—than in all the poetry since Milton."

One settles into George Herbert. Poetic pyrotechnics matter far less than spiritual process. I missed this point in graduate school. Not only was I reading poetry in the wrong spirit, I also missed the relevance of the best criticism. Come back to T. S. Eliot, who has quite a bit to say about the *function* of "metaphysical" verse. George Herbert, Eliot explains in my drab black-and-white textbook, offers:

> the personal record of a man very conscious of weakness and failure, a man of intellect and sensibility who hungered and thirsted after righteousness. And that by its content, as well as because of its technical accomplishment, is a work of importance for every lover of poetry.

Set aside (if you can) the dated sexism of Eliot's language—"a man of intellect," a "man very conscious of weakness." His broader observation about a hunger or thirst for "righteousness," about wanting to be a better person, provides a valid takeaway—far more important than ego-driven rankings. As I consumed poetry for the wrong reasons in grad school, so too did I miss on intent. For years, I got distracted by Eliot's laddish rearrangement of the literary trophy cabinet; I never noticed what he really had to offer the "lover of poetry." I overlooked his conclusion that an authorial search, not just the "technical accomplishment," should drive our assessment.

And here is why people come out of graduate programs in literature so messed up. We misdiagnose ourselves with doctorates. Every reader I know struggles with silence in some way. We're after something in our lives that the standard plot lines cannot provide. Some story that the dominant culture will not disclose. Literature does not offer a path so much as a surrogate or echoing voice, a way of hearing parts of ourselves cut off by cruder narratives. We may start out listening for the hidden story lines, then we get distracted. Our training focuses on the externals. As a consequence, we miss the point of our own quest.

In my case, literature became a job. The job became my life. None of this was healthy. Chasing full-time positions after graduate school, Julie and I moved to Philadelphia, then to Georgia, Florida, and Mississippi, then back again to Florida. Slowly I had to unlearn the bad habits I picked up during an imperfect education; I needed to recover what took me to literature in the first place, why I initially enrolled in a graduate class on seventeenth-century poetry.

With each new city or town, Julie and I have claimed a bit more space for ourselves. We continue to travel back into our past. We try out what used to work, retool what still has use, and discard what corrodes. Along the way, we define home. "No more, 'I will abroad!'" We listen for what the radically peaceful Quakers describe as a still, silent voice. "Methought I heard one calling, *Child*!" We hunger for contentment. "And I replied, *My Lord*." We seek quotidian truths, not drama, but a freedom from undue bias or self-generated contempt. We long for the happy neighborhood. We need peace at home.

Memory Care, from some lines
by Andrew Marvell

But ours so truly parallel,
Though infinite, can never meet.
                    —Andrew Marvell, "Definition of Love"

It took me by surprise,
though it should not have,
how my son said he
wanted me out of his life,
fulfilling the prophecy
of the social worker
who cautioned how
I should reconcile feelings
about my own father
before taking in a child,
for I too have longed
to end a relationship,
at least since that moment
when I agreed to paint
my father's den, dad
then too old to paint
the room himself.
"Don't drip on the floor,"
he warned, leaving me
feeling humiliated
and small, as if
I had traveled
by bus across two
states to splatter
paint on his rug.
That story lay inert
in subconscious muck

until one morning
when I pressed
the elevator button
for the second floor,
Memory Care,
at the facility where
my father then lived,
and where his furniture
had been laid out,
if on a smaller scale,
in the very room
I painted ten years
before, and where
my father would now
greet me, wearing
an old t-shirt, black
socks, and navy blue
scoop-crotch briefs.
I offered to help him
put on pants since
he had a guest, but
he said "I'm content"
then proceeded to
position himself
on the bed at such
an angle that I had
no choice but to eye
his navy blue, scoop-
crotch briefs. We talked,
or I tried my best to talk,
though I felt more cognizant
of the clock that marks
a respectable visit's end,
and just before that very
moment when I could
excuse myself, dad

declared "I'm tired,"
pulled on pants,
walked me down
the hall, then left,
and while waiting
for the nurse to code
me down to the lobby,
I did not feel sad at all.
I understood my son
for once. I blessed
the dementia that let
me wish another
man dead.

Apologia, for my father

I'm sorry for writing about you, you would have loved it—

every juicy detail, every kernel of sweetened truth, the now-public "can you believe that?" whisper to the whole affair, from the seamy trysts at a Darien B&B to the craven fantasy that, if you could only hold out until the cancer was done, you would helm her departed husband's yacht;

and on top of your fifteen-year side job, the philandering, the harassment of secretaries who got fired or left in disgust, vanished from your memory like abandoned box cars;

then in your sixties, *your sixties!*, an Asian mistress whom you picked up on the Stamford local;

and I'm sorry this poem just took a racist turn for I failed to mention how the first woman was white, as in white-right-and-uptight (but what is it about Republican men and their Asian girlfriends—and what ever compelled you to share with me details about your "rough sex"?);

and I'm sorry to say this, but in some fundamental ways, you were a shitty dad;

for I doubt you felt sorry about Mom's arrhythmia; truth be told, her heart improved when she left you—she's doing fine now, not that I can even ask (my only task now being to pray you across this suburban bardo);

and that said, I'm sorry for what I wrote, for spilling the beans, for speaking my truth, for airing dirty laundry, I hate that song, I'm sorry for letting this angry cat out of the bag, I'm sorry for my cowardice;

and I'm sorry on behalf of all Creation that you could not have been born unto some far-off time and place, where it would have been perfectly acceptable for a man to lie in bed while the first wife unpeels his overripe banana and a second fixes breakfast,

56

but that is not the space-time continuum, not the patriarchal
    porn flick, we happen to inhabit;
and I'm sorry, I really am, that you sought the trappings of Victorian
    family, a public virtue to gloss the inner emptiness, a moral
    compass gifted from Ronald Wilson Reagan to Roger Stone,
    you wanted to be the dad your own father never lived to be;
and I'm sorry if I wrote too much, if I have betrayed some family
    trust, and I apologize sincerely for secretly, cynically recording
    every sordid detail in my own memory bank, because as a writer,
    I knew that I would one day turn your story unto my own ends;
and I'm sorry that dementia took you before this book got published,
    which, truth be told, I never could have written until you were
    dead;
I'm sorry if you come across as an affectionate yet amoral man-child,
    but at least you're the center of attention, where you always
    wanted to be, still suffocating me, perhaps your other kids as
    well (who knows?);
and I'm sorry you'll never be able to read what I wrote.
You would have loved it.

What We Pass Down, also for my father

You killed the first act:
Cub Scouts, coaching
little league, family

vacations across
country, loading
up the car, driving

driving, driving
until we saw it all.
Then you stopped.

What happened? Did kids
hold your interest only
when you were in charge,

when your words could
carry the Gregory Peck
gravitas before a young

and admiring Scout?
(Not the teenage punk
who stopped listening.)

If I could play back
the years, knowing
what I know now,

I would tell you that
being a father is
much like being

Thomas Hallock

the training wheels
on a child's first bike,
bouncing, scuffling

down the sidewalk,
new abrasions scarred
onto the plastic wheel

with each bump
against the concrete.
Then we go away.

The wheels get tossed
into the garage—never
entirely forgotten.

"Are you even listening,"
my own son asks me.
And I am, processing

household knowledge,
this love which forms
the sum of our days.

How my wife likes
chocolate, but not
chocolate chip cookies.

"You say that like
it is something new,"
my own kid responds.

And it's true, I live
too much inside my
own head, forgetting

my mother's birthday,
eating the last slice
of pizza, drinking

the half cup of milk
which my son had
saved for morning.

On Hypotext, or how scripture got rewritten by the Chicago Seven

Any text is a hypertext, grafting itself onto a hypotext, an earlier text that it imitates or transforms; any writing is rewriting; and literature is always in the second degree.
> —*Gerald Prince, from the foreword to Gérard Genette,*
> Palimpsests: Literature in the Second Degree *(1997)*

But whosoever shall deny me before men, him will I also deny before my Father which is in heaven.
> —*Matthew 10:33*

For I am come to set a man at variance against his father....
> —*Matthew 10:35*

We have this confusion of fathers.
A crisis. Which will it be?
If you, our Savior, sets man
at variance against the father,
what do we make of the same
acquiescence before your own?
I mean, who made *you* the exception?
And what happens to Joseph, vanishing
from the story altogether? Why trust
these truths that cannot close themselves?

When Abbie Hoffman took the stand
I was just four, still learning to talk.
Both of my parents voted for Nixon.
My mother was in the kitchen,
three kids on the floor, cooking up
one more. The sixties did not happen.
So tell me, Rebbe, what should we feel

61

for that lost stepfather of goyish law,
the elderly Judge Hoffman, swallowing
hard at Yiddish jokes he actually caught.

The gavel bangs amidst threats of contempt,
an irreverent dance of chapter and verse,
anger not at the surface but at the source,
a long-haired, prodigal dope-smoking punk
in gleeful variance with the federal bench.
A father recognizes the breach. It's how
white men think, presuming scripture
to be fixed, all meaning stable and set,
fearing the glacial melt of hypotext.

My father was right to feel the affront.
He served in Korea, he worked all week,
raised the kids whenever he could, posed
for pictures on Christmas morn. What use
did he have for the shuffling of scripture
Leave archetypes be! Why shift the bounds
of meaning? He longed for eternal Law—
but Jesus, what I now seek are variants,
a freedom from the smug recitations
of Paul, a provenance thawed by hypotext.

On Some Problems Translating the *Naufragios* of Álvar Núñez Cabeza de Vaca, Good Friday 1528

Cernícalo. Avecilla de rapiña; especie de gavilán bastardo, con que suelen entretenerse los muchachos, haciéndoles venir a tomar la carne de la mano.
—*Sebastián de Covarrubias Horozco,* Tesoro de la Lengua Castellana o Española

The next day the governor raised standards on behalf of Your Majesty and took possession of the country in your Royal name. He showed his credentials and was acknowledged as governor according to Your Majesty's commands. We likewise presented our titles to him and he complied, as was required.
—*Álvar Núñez Cabeza de Vaca, "How We Arrived in Florida" (1528), translated by Fanny Bandelier*

Windfucker. 1. A name for the kestrel: cf. WINDHOVER. 2. fig. as a term of opprobrium. —Oxford English Dictionary

Windfucker (noun, obsolete):
a kestrel and a curse,
the smallest of raptors,
those who delight in
or manipulate words.

El Cernícalo, bastard
sparrowhawk, entertains
young boys by taking meat
from their small hands
(Covarrubias, *Tesoro*).

After the Requerimiento,
the governor turned
to the scrivener who

notarized the claim.
All papers were in order.

A congestive panther
stalks rabbits and field
mice along the prairie's
edge. Who knows what
usages get stolen next?

Covarrubias, kestral.
Courtesy Universidad Complutense de Madrid

Poetic Life in Dog Years (a pentimento)

Anyone who goes to art museums has a favorite pentimento. It doesn't matter whether you even know the technical term; you get the concept. "Pentimento," from the Italian for "repentance." As the *Grove History of Art* explains, "Visible evidence of an alteration to a painting or drawing that suggests a change of mind on the part of the artist"; the "previous workings" on a canvas, often more visible with age, as the "thin layers of paint that were originally opaque [become] semi-transparent." My favorite pentimento is a John Singer Sargent at the Metropolitan Museum of Art, *Madame X*. In this full-length portrait, Madame Pierre Gautreau confidently fronts the viewer, challenging Victorian reserve with her plunging black velvet evening gown. At first showing the portrait's jeweled strap trailed off a voluptuous bare shoulder; the family was scandalized, however, leading Sargent to re-secure the diamond strap safely above the repentant subject's notched scapula. Prudery won the day. In Jan van Eyck's *Arnolfini Portrait* at London's National Gallery, a convex mirror in center back hints to more than what we can see on the finished surface. The husband in this wedding portrait has wonky hands. And who is the cloudy figure in the mirror? An X-ray reveals the hands' repositioning—an inside joke, perhaps, maybe the hint to a backstory? We'll never know for certain. Pentimenti move us through their mystery. In a Houston chapel, Mark Rothko's brooding, bruised maroons morph and turn, vanish and reappear under a black sheen, shifting unpredictably under carefully filtered overhead light.

I feel silly alluding to these works myself. They are masterpieces, rightly enshrined in our high temples of the Aesthetic. But anyone who dabbles with art, in any form, recognizes how personal drama underlies the creative process. Sculptors, painters, photographers, illustrators, musicians, writers, and the rest "cover up" the evidence of prior drafts. A minor detail may say too much, challenge

John Singer Sargent, *Madame Pierre Gautreau* (1884),
as shown at the 1884 Paris Salon.

Image copyright © The Metropolitan Museum of Art / Image source: Art Resource, NY

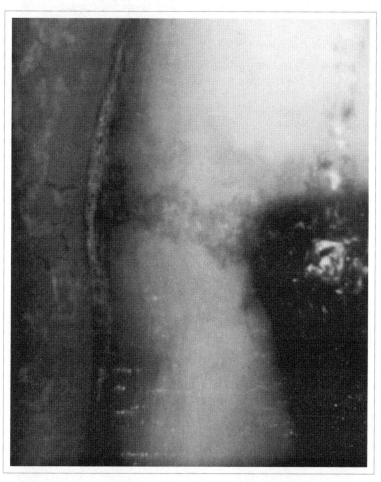

An infared reflectogram detail of the finished painting carries traces
of the diamond strap off Gautreau's right arm, under the paint applied
later. Technical studies indicate that the strap was above the shoulder on
a first draft; then off the arm in the 1884 version; and after controversy,
safely notched back above the shoulder, where it rests today.

Image copyright © The Metropolitan Museum of Art / Image source: Art Resource, NY

propriety, or broach polite taste. Or sometimes just the opposite occurs, as the process gives the creator courage to disclose more, to travel further. Who knows? Pentimenti cannot be explained on practical terms. I imagine Jan van Eyck saying "no" to a do-over; he would *not* redraw those exquisite oranges on the Arnolfini windowsill. Or maybe, as in Sargent's case, there was an easy fix (scrape away the oil paint and reposition a dress strap). With Rothko, the process was the point. Julie and I recently caught a solo show at our hometown Museum of Fine Arts that featured textile portraits by the Bahamian artist Gio Swaby; Swaby, whose mother was a seamstress, would leave the thread showing in her machine-sewn portraits. The display of work honored the worker. A pentimento points to the search.

And that leads me to the four poems below.

Our image of the writer in popular movies invariably shows the trash can surrounded by wadded yellow scrap paper. That's not my case. Call it narcissism, but I rarely throw out drafts. When working towards something, I print the newest version and clip it on top of the previous one. I don't look at the earlier drafts, but that's not my point. Writers strip away; that's what we do.

Take my dad. He was a loving but confused man, caring in his own way, on his terms, generous though emotionally stunted, controlling to the point of abusive. Julie battled with him openly; my struggles were subterranean. When I first started writing poems about my father, the process turned awkwardly, like a stripped slotted screw. The first two drafts, coming from angry isolation, started with morning walks to the park, where I watched the sun rise and meditated, trying to catch some peace for myself. A third, on the aging of my canine companion Virgil, peeked around time's corner when I became a father myself. And a fourth, which started on the maudlin subject of a dying dog, shifted its attention to my father, who despite his outward gregariousness died alone. Or maybe, I should be more specific. My dad died in the presence of a hospice nurse. He always felt most comfortable around strangers. Safer that

An infrared reflectogram of *The Arnolfini Portrait* by
Jan van Eyck showing revisions, including the repositioning of
Giovanni Arnolfini's waving right hand.

Detail of an infrared reflectogram of the
The Arnolfini Portrait by Jan van Eyck showing revisions.
Courtesy, The National Gallery, London

way, I guess—to cut yourself off. The choice is private, how we die,
though a bad precedent to pass on to your son.

And so these poems, pentimenti, from first to final drafts,
which for reasons I cannot fully explain myself, cohere around the
same binder clip:

I.

Before the print lives, before
the obligations or newspaper
politics occupy your mind,

start out for a park, some place
where water meets land. Face East,
not like Pizzaro, for true empires

have always looked toward the sun
and we have forgotten our animal
sense, sure as our own names.

How many of us can still trace
the stories of the constellations?
Who left the porch light on?

If you need an advocate, one
will be provided: A band of
umber brims above the horizon.

The sun is a morning star, the origin
of all poems, more accommodating
than Polaris, and all you need to know.

II.

Lost in the sky, the moon sets at sunrise.
Day breaks with the crack of a dozen eggs.

White pelicans wheel over Tampa Bay
while the yellow moon, lost in the sky,

traces its ludic, transcendental arc,
banded by borrowed light, crazy full,

a drunken outlier to our hourly lives
slowing the happy neighborhood.

I have done my mental calisthenics,
lost myself in morning time;

the dog is walked, coffee made,
I have one thing left to do:

wake my son, take him outside
to see this moon, lost in the sky.

III.

Too old to reach the park, he remains
content to patrol the yard, and I too

must adjust, with no more morning
walks to observe how the sun diffuses

its cool light across the bay, where I can
count my breaths and enumerate my days.

You fulfilled your charge, Virgil,
upholding your illustrious name

and from your cloudy stare, I now
will take your lessons home—

how life is short, and love must be long,
and why every father must have a dog.

IV.

First the hips. You pause at the stairs,
bark less, take longer naps. Now this.
Even after a long walk, I watch
my step. That was a nice rug.

You reached me mezzo cammin
but a dog's life is shorter than ours,
so you guide us on how to live,
then how to die. On my father's

last night, I should have stayed. With
each wet cough, I looked up. Around
two a.m., I went home. Gregarious
but remote, he died alone.

Part Three

Family and Home

Chicken Aubade

The complaints, the clucks,
the ovulating squawks

remind me of the hawk
that we saw

in the yard. It hunts
at daybreak.

Thirty minutes, please,
Julie is sleeping.

Invocation

—for Julie

I cleaned out the pen you gave me,
a Waterman, *noir*, made in Nantes,
a gift we could not afford
at the time, one I had resolved
to save for poetry, though
I had forgotten my practice
and the unused ink had run dry.
So I unscrewed the pen's casing,
ran hot water down the beveled nib,
blew through the hollow orifice
like it was some absurd duck call
to dislodge any of the loose crud,
then I soaked the dismembered
stylus in a coffee mug by the sink,
and flushed the clear ink cartridge
(my instructions say *réservoir*)
by spinning the threaded dial
clockwise then counterclockwise,
plunging the rubber gasket
through the plastic *réservoir*
until the expired ink had
stained the kitchen sink
with its exquisitely unread
azure plumes. And as the parts
dried on an unused coffee filter,
I found a sheet of notebook
paper I had forgotten about,
left folded under the white satin
lining of the navy blue box,
a to-do list from Christmas,
with the reminder to buy
a sweatshirt for my father

who got cold at his facility.
He died a year ago that February.
I threw away the obsolete list
and reassembled my pen,
which had stained the coffee
filter a deep indigo. But
still, the pen would not write,
though mostly it was me.
I scribbled out a poem
that had worked last night
at three a.m. but felt forced
in the light of day, for even
though I had relied on stanzas,
using meter's handrail to ease
my way back into verse,
the conceit felt maudlin,
even the slant rhymes
would not land. So I set
my pen back into its box
and waited until next morning,
when fumbling through
the same pre-dawn darkness,
I settled upon a second
conceit to hang my tired
thoughts, and though
the nib still scratched
through the pages
of my cheap tablet,
I found that if I wrote
more slowly, pressing
firmly onto the page,
the lines obliged me,
flowing somewhat,
still, like a redemptive
river of indigo ink.

Interlude

Patriarchy Meets the Man-Eating Goddess

My mother called early one October morning, some twenty years ago. "Your father and I are getting a divorce," she said. "He's been having an affair for fourteen years and I've known about it for four. We were seeing a marriage counselor but he no longer goes. So I made my decision. We've been together forty years but that is enough."

A strange three weeks followed. When my mother presented the news to him, my father appeared to be so devastated (she explained) that even I could not have left him alone. He promised to change and said that the affair was winding down anyway. My mother agreed to reconcile; the slightest contact with this woman, however, and the marriage was over.

Of course, the affair continued. My parents compromised and my mother swallowed her pride. On the surface, they enjoyed a good life. As compensation for a marriage without trust, my parents lorded over a recently restored Victorian home. Their backyard adjoined a tidal estuary off the Long Island Sound—space they shared with nesting waterfowl, fiddler crabs, and, of course, the bank. My parents traveled, enjoyed dinner with the neighbors, weekends at Karen and Bill's, Super Bowl parties at the Browns'. A divorce, my mother thought, would bring devastating changes to a woman in her sixties. Divorce meant losing her house, maybe even her friends.

It did not work out that way. When the news broke, everybody seemed to know the story already, even if details of the revelation were new, and friends especially took my mother's side. Regardless, divorce did not fit the life-plot that shaped my parents' generation. They came from a pre-Brady Bunch world, where the man played it the company way while the mother raised the kids. Even as the early seventies showed cracks in the bourgeois façade—Adrienne Rich dove into the wreck and Sylvia stuck her head in the oven—my mom and dad skipped the Women's Movement and Viet Nam protests, they never inhaled, they bypassed the counterculture and proceeded directly to Reagan.

After the threat by my mom to leave, and a retaliation by my father in the form of silenced wounding, the relationship carried on as before. My parents visited Julie and me in Georgia, Valdosta to be specific, where we found jobs after graduate school. During my parents' visit, the family reverted to formal breakfasts. Every dish we owned got used. A new plate for bacon and eggs, saucers for coffee cake, separate bowls for the grapefruit, a pitcher for the milk, cloth napkins and two kinds of spoons. After we ate, my father would stack the dishes in the center of the table, clear space around him, then unfold my copy of the *Valdosta Daily Times*. Manners kept me from allowing someone else to bus our table (certainly my wife Julie would not), so I took his dirty plates to the sink, knowing that since I was already in the kitchen, he would ask me to top off his coffee as well. These were the minor indignities that pushed a generation to Washington for bra burnings and pro-choice marches. My mother missed those; she retaliated instead with a wicked wit. My father claims her sarcasm drove him to another woman.

Emotional strain registered itself through language—then and now.

Back in Valdosta we had some magnet poetry on the side of our refrigerator. Before my parents came to visit, Julie spelled out this declaration of woman's lib:

I am a man eating goddess
lather me
lie with me
worship me

The piece is why I love my wife. She is an occasional Riot Grrrl who manages to combine second-and-one-half wave feminism with a dose of southern womanhood. And she has a good ear to boot.

But something strange happened with my parents' visits. While they were in town, the poem kept disappearing. The first time, Julie found it brushed back into the babble of unused magnets. She blamed one of our cats and reordered the words. When the poem disappeared again, she linked suspect and crime. Julie set the scene for the third visit, clearing away any stray language, so the words "I AM A MAN EATING GODDESS" were unmistakable. A couple of days later, true to script, "lather" and "ly" from the next stanzas were lifted from the older poem and drafted under a new line, "raw power can rip a boy."

Julie pounced on the scene. "Been writing some poetry," she asked my father. My dad said he hadn't touched her work—or if he did, it was accidental. He resented the accusation. An argument ensued. My father was all denial. He would not believe that he had appropriated someone else's language, even as he held an incriminating magnet between finger and thumb.

The denial was pathological—providing we define pathology as social category rather than as individual ailment. The customs of patriarchy would allow my father to avoid a truth: that in his silly little exercise, even if unwittingly, he had stolen a woman's words. He felt no need to apologize. The changes on our refrigerator represented one of those silent rumblings of power in male-female relations, the kind that don't show up on spousal Richter scales but that shape lives nonetheless.

The earlier revisions had been passed by without comment, and if no one commented, then the theft of words never happened. One of the best strategies for avoiding a rejection of patriarchy (even with magnet poetry) is to deny that there had even been a story to tell. The declaration "I am a man eating goddess" turned what is ordinarily a playful space into one where voices are defined, appropriated, contested, and defended.

The poet Gloria Anzaldúa has quite a bit to say about god-
desses, silencing, blood sacrifice, and giving voice to women. Her
hybrid book *Borderlands/La Frontera* traces out a genealogy of the
virgin of Guadalupe, known by her Indian name as Coatlalopeuh,
who was also a central Native deity and who remains a taproot for
Mexican people to this day. The recovery of a poetic voice, for
Anzaldúa, involves this connection with Coatlalopeuh in a way that
had been previously silenced: first by a male-dominated Aztec-Mexica culture that drove Mayan deities underground, then by the Cath-
olic Church.

Coatlalopeuh descends from an earlier incarnation of a Mesoamerican fertility goddess, from Coatlicue or "serpent skirt." But the
Aztec-Mexica religious-military state split the deity, leaving To-
nantsi as the good mother and taking the serpent/sexuality out of
her. This division, which began with the Aztec-Mexica invasion of
the Nahua people, evolved into a present-day dichotomy between
Guadalupe, the chaste protective mother, and Coatlicue, *la puta*.
Anzaldúa seeks to undo this dichotomy. In writing, she explains:

> I see *oposición e insurrección*. I see the crack growing on the
> rock. I see the fine frenzy building. I see the heat of anger
> or rebellion or hope split open that rock, releasing *la Coat-
> licue*. And someone in me takes matters into our own
> hands, and eventually, takes dominion over serpents—over
> my own body, my sexual activity, my soul, my mind, my
> weaknesses and strengths. Mine. Ours. Not the heterosex-
> ual white man's or the colored man's or the state's or the
> culture's or the religion's or the parent's—just ours, mine.

The consciousness of a new mestiza demands the recovery of language. It heals the *puta/virgen* split, reuniting Coatlalopeuh and
Coatlicue: "I will have my tongue—my woman's voice, my sexual
voice, my poet's voice. I will overcome the tradition of silence." For
Anzaldúa, this arrival to consciousness holds mortal stakes. The av-
erage life span of a Mexican farm laborer is 56; her father died at 38.

Anzaldúa's mythology of *la frontera* may seem distant from my parents' Long Island Sound. But we all fight different battles of spirit and silence. A year or so before moving to Valdosta, Julie and I attended a Mother's Day service at the Unitarian-Universalist Church in Philadelphia. It was the church where we got married. The sermon that morning was on domestic violence. An ex-nun named Joan and our minister Holly, one-half of a husband/wife team, spoke to the congregation. They began by reviewing some of the chilling statistics on domestic abuse, proceeding slowly and punctuating each fact with the beat of a drum. Ordinarily, the prospect of two white women drumming from the pulpit would have sent me toward the exit, and had I known the topic, I would have stayed home. But there were stories I still need to acknowledge. According to the National Coalition of Domestic Violence, Holly stated:

- A battering crime occurs in this country every fifteen seconds. *Boom.*
- Over fifty percent of all women will experience violence in a domestic relationship. *Boom.*
- One-third of all women who visit an emergency room are there for injuries related to ongoing abuse. *Boom.*
- One in five of all pregnant woman are battered. *Boom.*
- One in four of all gay couples experience domestic violence in their relationships. *Boom.*
- Sixty percent of all disabled women (by conservative estimate) have experienced sexual abuse. *Boom.*
- Over two-thirds of all female victims of violence knew their attackers. *Boom.*
- Divorced and separated women make up seven percent of the United States population, but they account for three-quarters of the women who have been battered. *Boom.*

The minister read each point in a clear and deliberate voice while Joan the ex-nun hit her drum. It was more than I could take. After the sermon, we sang "Spirit of Life," one of those god-awful holdovers from the seventies that UU's insist on singing, and against this backdrop of musical macramé, I started crying.

The night before, my sister had mentioned over a second pitcher of beer that our mom was on heart medication. I had never faced the mortality of a parent before and the news caught me off guard; at an unconscious level the statistics connected to my mother's irregular heartbeat. My mother has a Scandinavian reserve, which means that she complains very little when she is upset, and the generation of marriage that she inherited compounded this tendency to swallow her thoughts. She is an enormously intelligent woman, a professional with an Ivy League degree, but one whose needs and career always fell second to domestic partnership and family. The relationship forged by my parents in the 1950s never moved beyond the seventies. That was her unspoken contract.

I cannot ever recall my father doing a load of wash. They talked over important decisions but the final say resided with him. Dinner was ready when the woman had prepared it. My mother traded autonomy for marriage, and the affair came as a blow to her self-respect. She suffered the indignity in silence—mostly. She retaliated with a sharp tongue that got only sharper, directing any leftover pain against herself; my father increasingly resented the sarcasm. Meanwhile they fronted the image of a happy relationship, one that had weathered a culture of divorce.

Consciously or not, I sensed that morning in church the violence in a betrayed marriage contract. After the divorce, my mother would emphasize the good things my father had done. He loved his children, he was proud of us all, he never lifted a hand against her. But the lying was a form of abuse. As she said over the phone, "I would rather he had thrown me down the steps."

I cannot stop thinking about the poem on the refrigerator. The words "I am a man eating goddess" stayed there long after my parents left. Only a trace of the prior conflict remains: the word "but," left after my parents' last visit, hanging at an odd angle, as if to suggest contingency to a feminist's half-playful declaration. The hint to personality clash, I think, added to the poem. It positions the words as a counterattack before the fact, the area of contest being language itself.

My father and I never discussed the damage done by his silent abuse while he was alive. Not openly—not in any real way. What I should have said is that relationships sour, that libidos wander, but the lying distanced him from the people he loves, from the people who need to love him. He relied on the weight of a patriarchal institution to hide the pain that his affair caused. The story of the old marriage plot did more harm than good. I had sensed the suffering before I knew the source.

Most of this essay was written before my mother called me about the divorce. (Language always creeps through the cracks.) Even after that, for decades, I tried to suppress what I had written. An earlier version of this piece appeared on a website called womenwriters.net, long defunct. Although I'm pretty compulsive about collecting my work, I never kept a printout or active link to the article. It's one of a handful of publications that I leave off my curriculum vitae, nor do include it on my university's archive of faculty publications. To locate the text, I had to use the "Wayback Machine," a tool for recovering abandoned websites, where one finds URLs after the Go Daddy payment has been missed.

I buried my own words. But like the lost spring under a Mesoamerican pyramid, the story bubbles up. My mother has said that she regrets mentioning the affair to anyone but my sister. "I should never have told you boys." But she did.

Anzaldúa encourages all of us to steel our nerve and undertake a similar journey. Each of us needs to look inside, examine the damage that patriarchy levels upon our lives. Male and female, gay and straight, black and brown and white, people in between—our times call for introspection. "People," Anzaldúa writes, "listen to what your jotería is saying." *What does your queerness want you to know?* What's in your wayback machine?

Heed the stories that refuse to close.

Hers

To select her own
heretical devotions,
to reject type, following
impolitic fossil bird tracks
across the scoured page—

Jonah was not
the Christ at all,
the whale spit him out,
wearied by the prophecies—

We hardly know code
so why digitize? Why
pay to have our words
shipped back to us from
a warehouse in Cincinnati?

The poet numbers her own
series, binding them herself,
throwing off the print life.
Not indifferent to fame,
she leaves hers to wait.

Florida Study

—for Gary Mormino

Come late February,
as the browning oranges
harden on their stems
and the morning light
streams off the bay
at such an angle
through the hearth
windows, as if
to create a forest
in our living room,
the heart pine glows.
I submit to the work
of stripping incarnadine
pink, white lead paint
then walnut stain
from the doorjambs
and trim, until each
amber plank, close
grained, unmarred
by knots, can better
recall the anonymous
flatwood from which
it came, taking us back
to a time now lost
to us in Florida, some
time that never was.

Thomas Hallock

Water Has Memory

Apart from our blunt indifference
to the most basic geographic terms,
terrace and swale, seepage and slope,
or to the vestigial lives of toponyms,
like how the homes along Lakeview Avenue
(or what is now 22nd Avenue South)
once overlooked an actual lake,
where limpkin (birds rare enough
to celebrate) now forage at marsh's
edge, near a city park that abuts the dump,
not coincidentally, on the Black side of town,
and in the same floodplain, or swale,
where garbage trucks haul
banana sweet mulch to dusty piles
that blow onto the playground
by the lake, and where, not by
coincidence but design, the
same dun-colored city trucks
once hauled the demolished home
of a troubled African-American man
named Hydra Lacy, who for reasons
I now forget climbed into the narrow
garret of his soon-to-be-widowed wife's
one-story home, and fired (back?)
at the cops, killing two men
and causing the police to retaliate
with such hair-trigger judgment
that they riddled the home with bullets
until (in my mind's eye) the pocked structure
collapsed under its own weight; in truth,
the house was bulldozed, but no matter,
say cop killer and reason evaporates—
before the feds could investigate

the city hauled away the rubble
to its waste facility by the park
on the lake, burying the ruins
of brick, sheetrock, mangled Romex
not too far from the swing sets
under a dirty cenotaph where
I now go to look for limpkin,
Tantalus ephouskyca, or crying bird
in Muskogean tongues, a species
that is finicky about habitat,
foraging upon a particular diet
of apple snail eggs that one would
not expect to find in a ditch
by the dump. My birding friends
are quick to correct me, saying
"you probably saw an immature ibis,"
and yes, point taken, limpkin do
have the same doe-like plumage
of a juvie ibis, though the latter's bill
curves like a scythe, limpkin are larger.
The problem is yours, I want to say,
because white people choose not
to look for nature on this side of town,
and either way, a cop killer's home
merits an investigation before
the city demolishes the site,
the mulch pile deserves a marker
of some kind because water has memory,
an unreconciled past never stops crying,
and I know what an ibis looks like.
I know a limpkin when I see one.

Thomas Hallock

Preparation, after Edward Taylor
(a poem to be read in performance)

I.

"Because of the sour milk and soda, this recipe has a very tender dough."
—*Irma S. Rombauer and Marion Rombauer Becker,*
Joy of Cooking *(1931)*

The secret to buttermilk
is the milk never sours,
so a carton wedged
into the back of the fridge
serves long after the whey
has settled on bottom.

> Sift together into a mixing bowl:
>> 1 3/4 cups sifted all-purpose flour
>> 1/2 teaspoon salt
>> 2 teaspoons double-acting baking powder
>> 1 teaspoon sugar
>> 1/2 teaspoon baking soda
> Cut in:
>> 1/4 cup of lard or 5 tablespoons butter
> Add and lightly mix:
>> 3/4 cup buttermilk

Alternatively:
Sniff, check for mold,
and shake the buttermilk;
stir in a cup of sifted
flour, a quarter stick
of chopped butter;
baking powder,
blend with the

wooden spoon
from your Aunt
Nell's kitchen.

(I prefer kneading with my bare
hands, I love to lick the sour,
tacky dough from my fingers—
that is not in the recipe book.)

   Place biscuits 1 inch apart if you like them crusty all over, close
together if not.
   Bake in a ▶ 450° preheated oven 12 to 15 minutes, depending
upon their thickness.

Yes: At 400 degrees
or higher, but bake
immediately,
because biscuits
transfigure
if allowed
to rise
while my
beloved
is sleeping.

II.

*"Once upon a time, when the English language was young, the word from which
the modern English 'lady' sprang meant 'loaf-kneader,' and the verb 'to knead'
has even prehistoric origins! To our own and our families' distinct profit—and
with little effort—we housewives can become 'ladies' again."*
       —*Rombauer and Rombauer Becker*, Joy of Cooking

*I am come into my garden, my sister, my spouse: I have gathered my myrrh with
my spice; I have eaten my honeycomb with my honey; I have drunk my wine
with my milk: eat, O friends; drink, yea, drink abundantly, O beloved.*
       —*Song of Solomon 5:1*

*Lady (noun). **Etymology:** < LOAF n.¹ + an otherwise unattested Old English
*dige, literally 'kneader' (compare DEY n.¹) < the same Germanic base as Gothic
digan to knead.*—Oxford English Dictionary

> There is a protocol
> to eating hot biscuits:
> the first is split in half and
> filled with veggie sausage or
> smeared with homemade mustard,
> that being the savory (or meal) biscuit,
> while the second is for dessert,
> best enjoyed with strawberry
> jam or the saw palm honey
> we bought yesterday
> at the market.

III.

*"This Bread of Life dropt in thy mouth, doth Cry.
Eate, Eate me, Soul, and thou shalt never dy."
—Edward Taylor, "I Am the Living Bread:
Meditation 8 (John 6:51)"*

*I am the living bread which came down from heaven: if any man eat of this
bread, he shall live for ever: and the bread that I will give is my flesh, which I
will give for the life of the world." —John 6:51*

> The mechanics of transubstantiation
> are vastly overrated, for is not a fresh
> biscuit also manna from heaven?

IV.

*"And they went up on the breadth of the earth and compassed the camp of the
saints about, and the beloved city: and fire came down from God out of heaven,
and devoured them." —Revelation 20:9*

"Does ripe fruit ever fall?" —Wallace Stevens, *"Sunday Morning"*

Let's skip church this morning,
uncrease the *Times* from
its thick fold and leave
the day to go its own way.

I will peel this orange
from our neighbor's yard
and pour you another cup
of coffee, my beloved:

I have laid these biscuits
on the broad plain
of our table, and together
we shall devour them.

Thomas Hallock

Prose Poem for the Epiphany

It is the relegation we must live with: how your favorite Spanish clogs, lime green in the catalog but more like fresh lima bean, green as in *te quiero verde*, how these beloved animal-friendly slides caught the attention of our near death, hyperannuated cat and maybe it was the smell, scent being the last of our senses to fade, or maybe it was spite, that we (you…me?) forgot to change the litter, because our pet children are like that. And why do adults without children talk about their pets as if domestic animals were people? Do human beings possess some innate need to care? Anyway, your shoes…ruined. No amount of buffing, not mink oil, nor saddle soap, not the juice from a lemon I pulled off the tree in our backyard this morning, can cut the jagged stink of urine. It is a burden we must live with, a suffering that behooves Jesus, whom the Gospels portray (not coincidentally) without shoes—in sandals, as it were. We wash ourselves clean with forgiveness. You don't wear sandals because your feet sweat, which means I can take this Christ parallel only so far, so I will drop the conceit, allusion is theory, but you get my point. The holidays are upon us and I secretly charged a pair of these same overpriced, organic strapless clogs, imported from the wine country of Rioja, just your size. Not to worry, we are almost out of debt. Forgive us this cat, shoes are just shoes, things are just things, and on the new day of giving, on this fresh green of Epiphany morn, your feet shall be shod once more.

Sonnets from Before and After Having a Kid

I. Before
It's not just how you pile the towel around
your hair as if it were a terry cloth crown
before you step out of the shower to
meet your most loyal subject, your true
devotee, the cat, who lies expectantly
for the morning rite of licking water
from your red toenails and feet—no, rather,
I feel strongly such tasks should fall to me.
Tell me, what exactly has this cat done?
Why is it you will trust the pets alone?

Call me jealous but if I could revise
the script, I would set your being beside
a bedside table, piled high with books filled
with milk and honey, with leaping gazelles,
I'd coax you into these folio sheets,
desert fresh off the line and perfectly
bound, for I am familiar with foolscap,
and we as one would explore Solomon's realm,
below the belly where your wheat lies heaped.
past that secreted mole, venturing well

Beyond the measure of all prior poems,
where hot-breath tropes shack up with similes
and Sir Philip Sidney slips Astrophel
the tongue. Let the cat seek his own rewards,
let us love like anniversary morn,
let limericks outlast epithalamia,
let seven years follow seven more,
seeking the things that only shepherds know,
inscripted in the tomb as sacred lore,
this bodily syntax, ours to unlearn.

Thomas Hallock

II. After

Woke from a dream about the man who
almost shot your mother decades ago
you leave the bed for a glass of water,
guiding yourself hand over hand along
the kicked off blankets and snoring dog,
following blind instinct and neural paths
that residual trauma cannot shake off.
And in this pre-dawn darkness you also
thought you heard our little boy cry out—
probably not, though you check to make sure.

The comforter lies tangled at his feet.
You tuck him in again with a kiss on
the cheek, even though he is already
asleep, and seeking stillness of some kind,
you pour yourself a glass of water by
the cool violet light of the fridge, you lie
on the couch and flip through a magazine
without reading. A raccoon trips the alarm
of our neighbor's hypersensitive car.
We are awake, you were never alone.

No story can erase what has been done;
while ten years have passed since you lost your mom,
dreams about Glenn Black still track through your head.
So come to me now, come, I offer you
comfort in bed, thread your way through darkness,
hand over hand, past the dog, the nightstand
piled high with these books we still have not read.
Let us rebind love's signature, pull the
fitted sheets past this weary tale of harm.
Return, sweet lamb, to the fold of my arms.

That a traffic light

is about half the size
of a small person
is a point widely known
though seldom expressed.
I mean, who hasn't noticed
a signal box outside
its functional context,
maybe at the now-closed
children's museum, where
the blinking red or green
prompted parents to remind
their kids when to stop,
when to cross, and
the point they are most
anxious to get across, that
we must always hold hands.
Or maybe you notice
one while waiting
for a booth at that chain
restaurant by the mall,
where on a dull Friday night
we mill by the entrance,
nursing watery beers,
filling the time with
meaningless small talk,
until the black plastic
LED pager flairs in
your visiting cousin's
cargo shorts, the hostess
Ashlee leads us to a still-
streaky table, and before
we all sit down, glancing
about the room, you notice

the size of a traffic light.
We all have such examples.
So it took me by surprise when
one morning after breakfast
you described to me how
a man was suspended
in a bucket truck over
22nd Avenue South,
doing electrical work,
and you remarked how
the light was almost half
the man's size. I bit my tongue
because, after twenty years,
I know how any conversation
can swing back around,
and sure enough,
just a few weeks later,
on a blustery morning
in early March,
a red light stopped me
at the same intersection.
I had just dropped off
our eight-year-old son
at elementary school,
the child I thought
we never would have,
a change late in life,
entirely unexpected,
this gift offered as unto
Abraham and Sarah,
and when a gust of wind
off Tampa Bay blew the
signal from its thin wire
into a bold, ephemeral serif,
like writing on the sky,
it confirmed for me

how marriages work,
how there is comfort
in a second cup of coffee,
how epiphanies operate
on their own time,
and I resolved to tell you
when I got home that,
yes, my beloved, traffic
lights really are much
larger than they appear.

Thomas Hallock

Lullaby

—also after Adaptation

Some orchids smell like chocolate,
    some are fetid, some are sweet—
the orchids in my front porch hammock
    lull me back to sleep.

        I bought this hammock at an unsigned shop
            off a side street in the Yucatán.
        When it smiles on my porch, the world
            blooms fresh tortillas once again,

                cenotes discharge their prayers,
                    circling clockwise around the Gulf;
              they filter tar balls in the sand, cleansing
                refineries in this dirty South.

                    The long red tide hits us hard,
                        leaving behind a waste of fish—
                  fruit flies swarm a cownose ray,
                      a bloated grouper rots on the beach.

                    The stench of death itches in my nose,
                      tourists complain they cannot swim,
                  they'll take their money somewhere else.
                      Without the sea, why stay here?

            Then a morning breeze blows off the bay,
                over relic dunes, through our house.
            I pull my hammock against the dawn
                until I no longer keep darkness out.

    I feed the cat, walk the dog, make
        breakfast, do the morning chores:
I'll wake our son, find clean socks,
        and just in time, get him off to school.

Some orchids smell like chocolate,
    some are citrus, tart and sweet—
the orchids from my magic hammock
    lulled me back to sleep.

State of the State

—for Rick Scott

Come August
evenings smell
like mildewed cloves.
Towering cumulus
pile over one another
all afternoon, blackening,
building, until they crack
like transmogrified slate.
And yet, the same evening
may distill itself into
the roseate yellow hue
of an eternal youth,
with a breeze
off the Gulf
kissing the skin
of dog walkers,
as if to say,
even though your
faculties have slipped,
the doctor said cataracts,
I can still give you this:
crickets tuning their songs
to the pooling shadows,
timed to the minute
as steam rises off
the concrete,
a screech owl
or red-shouldered
hawk, the blithe fact
that nature does not care,
you will die, in spite
of who you voted for,

our governor is a crook,
and the cumulus clouds will
repeat their daily drama,
the lightning will still
crack, the holy cycle
will repeat itself,
just as the rain
shall fall again,
tomorrow.

City House Poem, a close

Swing open the blue gate,
carefully, nudge the front
edge over the loose brick,

for the latch does not close
cleanly. The top and bottom
hinges were not set square.

Precision never was my forte.
I love this garden, though
hardly anything is straight.

The coontie in the corner,   *Zamia pumila*
one leaf from a starchy root,
will take over someday.

I started with cocoplum,   *Licania michauxii*
thinking sand hills and scrub,
but it needed more sun.

We have an unworkable
plot, a xeric hammock
over sterile relic dune,

where even the hardwoods
hunger for hurricanes, water
runs straight through the sand

and still, these mosquitoes!
No one recognizes this noble
procession of humble plants.

The marlberry, with its waxy   *Ardisia escallonioides*

Thomas Hallock

leaves and black-blue berries,
feed the fattening robins, who

arrive each February, just
before their migration North.
They remember our place!

Yaupon holly, a privilege,   *Ilex vomitorium*
a royal drink, our native
source of caffeine, standing

just a little bit too close
for my tastes to the
statue of St. Francis.

Past the second gate our sea
grapes arc toward infinity—   *Coccoloba uvifera*
I've been working on that line.

Tread carefully in back, where
the bulging live oak root   *Quercus virginiana*
has cracked the sidewalk.

The lower limbs compete
with the firebush, which   *Hamelia patens*
I am still trying to reshape

after this bush got mauled
by the roofers (swallowtails
love its gaudy sweet flower).

Each plant, each feature,
a chapter from our lives.
We share this planet.

Spin the prayer wheel
I built after our pilgrimage
to the Mongolian steppe.

The wooden bench, from
a cedar slab our son
salvaged from the dump.

The kumquat tree from his first
Christmas, replacing the
loss from his foster home.

Fortuna sp.

How you fuss at me when I use
the retired trowel in the bed
I built when your mother died!

The pond, so you can hear water
while eating breakfast, the hibiscus
also native, from the St. Johns,

Hibiscus coccineus

remember Bartram's watercolor—
there is a story or soul to every
curious plant he ever drew.

The holly, from a charity auction,
it was the last scraggly specimen
waiting for a bid, now it competes

Ilex opaca

with the sprawling wild coffee
which I can hardly get rid of,
which all but propagates itself,

Psychotrias nervosa

each spring yielding new
volunteers from its plump jet
berries, overtaking all order.

Small wonder I cannot
find the line. I know you
wanted something cleaner.

This yard, an unruly mess,
the unnatural concoction
of green thoughts misled.

The butterfly orchid in our   *Encyclia tampensis*
live oak, also endangered,
described here, not too far

from our happy neighborhood—
its roots took to the furrowed
bark as if the flower never left.

I know, I know, I keep
losing control, even
the tercets escape me—

no meter, no music, no
rhythm, no rhyme. This
garden is but homespun,

sum of countless evenings
digging after dark, then
showing up for dinner

in a t-shirt smeared in mulch
and sweat. I break off a piece
of bread from the loaf you

just pulled from the oven,
without washing my hands,
and you rightly chastise me.

But can I show you one
more thing? Come back
to the porch, just a sec,

watch the loose plank
on the second step, yes,
I will replace it, along

with the landscape light
when we redo the deck—
maybe add some screen,

no, no idea where the bugs
come from. See how darkness
falls in an endless increase.

We are lucky to live where we do,
it is the cracked window into
a paradise of our own design.

Slide open the blue door, close
it again, fast with the latch
where our hands have worn

away the old paint. We've
paid this property off. Let's
in. The evening is ours.

Thomas Hallock

Conclusion

Camper Van

A pandemic is not the time to kick out one's child.

I forget the trigger. Or was it a cause? (Because trigger and cause are easily confused, leading as they do to the same end.) The kid said he wished I was dead. Or that I should jump off a bridge. That he did not have to listen to me. Maybe I heard one too many "fuck you's." Maybe he threatened to punch me in the gut again. Honestly, I do not remember the cause. Or the "trigger," as it were. I only remember that I kicked him out.

This was not the ending to the story that Julie and I had in mind.

Just two months before, our son had left for college. While he was never a conscientious student, going back to school seemed like a good idea. Then the coronavirus hit. Classes moved to an online format. The pandemic rendered a fragile situation impossible. Already flunking before Covid-19, the kid tendered no effort toward online learning. At home, he scarcely budged from the bed. He moved only to eat, use the bathroom, or roam the streets at the very, very wee hours of the morning.

Our son had never wanted to come back home. He liked the freedom from his parents in college. After a few months apart, he no longer wanted to be treated like a child. The terms had changed. The landscape had shifted. The kid would not be told to wash his crusty dishes, shut the lid of a filthy toilet, or throw away week-old chicken bones. But when trash started piling around a garbage can, spilling from the container to a pile on the floor, I broke.

"You have to leave," I told our son. He did not move off his mattress.

I escalated, tossing his suitcase and clothes out the door. He needed to find somewhere else to live, I screamed.

105

Then the kid surprised me. He left. He texted a friend, who had a job and a studio apartment, and made arrangements for himself. The friend's girlfriend was coming over Sunday; until then, the kid could stay there. With barely a word, he packed the stuff I had thrown into the yard, walked to the curb, and calmly vowed that we would not hear from him again.

At least through the weekend.

This was not my finest parental moment. During the pandemic's early months, I should not have pushed a teenage child with strict demands. It was dangerous.

Family members and friends tried talking me down from my rage. We were in the first weeks of a quarantine. Restaurants, parks, and gatherings of all kinds were closed. Without work, the kid had no way of supporting himself. Covid-19 deaths were already stacking up like crossed tallies in New York City and health officials predicted Florida to be the site of the next catastrophe. Everyone I knew had already lodged themselves in virus-free shelters. It was not the time to take in someone else's unemployed, sloppy teen. I was basically consigning a child to homelessness.

On Monday, however, my son was back. He came home and dumped his dirty laundry on the floor. I should expect no apology, he declared. The kid felt no remorse for the cursing, or the mess, the threat to punch me in the gut, or whatever shit that may come out of his mouth. What was I going to do? We were stuck.

And that's what brings me to the camper van.

The previous January, Julie and I bought a 1987 Volkswagen Westfalia. We spent far more on this vehicle than we should have, but when my dad passed away, he had left enough money for a frivolous purchase. My father loved life's small pleasures (a little too much!) and he would have approved of this particular find. Julie's mother had died of Alzheimer's, a year before my father, and for the first time in fifteen years we had no one to care for. No parents and the kid graduated. The only happiness we needed to tend to was our own.

I bought the camper van in Atlanta. My son and I flew up to close the purchase on the last Friday of December. We met the reluctant seller at his office by the airport. I gave him a check, he gave me the keys, and we switched out license plates. The kid and I drove the van back down from Georgia on the first of the new year.

It was a long, exquisite drive. The Westfalia was built for a speed limit of 55 and I did not yet feel comfortable with the interstate. So we followed Highway 41, lumbering through southern Georgia, then north Florida—past fallow fields of cotton and soy, peach groves then pecan. It was one of the few peaceful days he and I have ever shared. We blasted rock and roll out the open windows in the Deep South, playing our music a little too loud, feeling safe, reckless, and just the right amount of wrong.

I am not the kind of person who purchases thirty-year-old, semi-reliable vehicles. My automotive decisions trend toward the cheap and functional. But Julie and I needed a change. The kid had made it through twelfth grade, and we hoped he would find his own path through college. Could we claim success?

Only one-third of the children who come out of the foster care system graduate from high school. Our son (thanks mostly to Julie) had already defied the heavy weight of prediction. We had cause for guarded optimism. The state pays college tuition for any adopted "special needs" kids, though it is the kind of legislation Florida specializes in—generous on the surface, though on closer inspection ineffectual and hollow, even callous. Only three percent of children in foster care actually earn a university degree. Rather than following the higher-ed path, far more wind up pregnant or homeless. With those areas, the state skimps. We are the product of cynical policy.

Our house bears the physical scars of Florida's dysfunction. There are holes in the plaster, doors that never shut right from slamming, dents in the molding—the physical toll of a little boy who was neglected when he was most vulnerable.

Julie and I bought the camper van because we needed something new. Our home held too much prior hurt. I needed a new project.

And a project I now owned. All clichés about German national character—orderly, systematic, logical, efficient—vanish with VW vans. The camper came loaded with gadgets, and through the first few weekends in January, I resolved to learn the quirks of this idiosyncratic vehicle. I parked behind the house and went to work. I read multiple instruction books. I tested the various knobs, switches, levers, hooks, and latches. For every feature or function that made sense, new questions appeared.

The roof cantilevers up, in a seemingly easy motion, though we quickly learned to be careful tucking the canvas inside its housing. The front passenger seat should be able to swivel around, turning the main cabin into a kind of living room. To unlock the seat and spin backwards, however, requires a hard pull on a hidden eye, and because the seat had not revolved in some time, the mechanism seemed unnecessarily stubborn. We struggled likewise with a bench seat in back, which should convert to a bed. To lay down the assembly requires a tug out, then a quick lift—the kind of move that depends on body memory, that cannot be explained in written instructions. I tried each hinge gently, knowing how many things in our home had been broken, and despite my care, with any random tug I would find myself holding a dismembered plastic part.

I have always avoided electrical work, which created more problems for me, because the van has a more complicated power grid than most homes. A three-pronged outlet on the left outside panel feeds a standard alternating current, while an auxiliary battery with an inverter gives temporary power. (The running engine recharges the auxiliary battery.) And I was initially excited about the solar panels, which the prior owner confessed he never used, though I am still not sure where they plug in.

Most of my learning came through fidgeting. I got to know my vehicle in no orderly way. Lights, motors, and small appliances cut off and on mysteriously, without reason or cause.

One Saturday afternoon, I looked for a plug to drain the water reservoir, which a logical design would have placed under the chassis. (It turns out that the tank drains through the sink.) Unbeknownst to me, when I started the engine, I also switched on the reservoir pump. At first I did not notice, because the van had not been plugged in. While out for a test drive, however, Julie detected a new noise.

"What's that sloshing sound," she asked.

I assumed we had everything turned off. Being somewhat deaf, I could barely hear my own blinker, much less water in the reservoir sink. With the engine running, I had switched on the pump, which (we would now learn) drains into the tiny sink.

We pulled over to investigate. I slid the side panel left. As the door opened, a cascade fell from the cabin floor, off the running board, over the curb and onto my feet. With the engine on, the spigot had started to spurt a slow but steady westphalian stream. I had flooded the cheap plywood cabinetry, auxiliary battery, and carpet. I panicked. What self-respecting German would locate a battery under the sink? Would the accident warp the laminate cabinets? Had I short-circuited our electrical system? I shut down the power and drove the camper van home. That night, I barely slept, fretting about the fried electrical system, mourning my father and the blown inheritance.

Eventually the problem worked out. We ran a fan overnight and dried the interior. The next day, I replaced the corroded battery, and when Julie and I pulled up the damp rug, we found another rug. Under the original carpeting happened to be rubberized flooring. So we yanked out the bottom layer, happy to have one less thing to rot or mildew. We lightened our load.

All of us could use a little candor in discussing our imperfections. I will never be an auto mechanic. The camper van poses challenges way above my skill set. We err in pushing ourselves too hard.

Here's an obvious rub with children: you cannot go back. A parent cannot undo the birth of a child—or in our case, an adoption. Every person who has ever raised a kid has also second-guessed the decision. (It would be inhuman not to.) The sane person will ask, at some point, *what was I thinking?* Social scientists have tried to quantify these doubts or explain the rationale. But even the most basic terms for investigation have proven to be impossible to frame. Psychologist Konrad Piotrowski (who looks at Poland, Germany, and the United States) sets the percentage of "parental regret" at one in every ten or eleven parents. The harder one's circumstances, the higher the chance of regret. Piotrowski cites several factors: a parent's own "adverse childhood experiences," poor "psychological and somatic health," unstable financial situation or home life, and the challenges of "children with special needs."

A handful of sociologists have asked flatly: if you could travel back in time, would you still have kids? The question defies easy answers, however. A stigma muzzles all but a handful of women—and besides, even if a parent regrets the decision, she or he still loves the kid. Our culture does not allow one to identify having children as a life-mistake. To declare misgivings about becoming a mother, the Israeli sociologist Lorna Donath writes, will cast the parent as a bad person. To give voice to the very thought, we believe, may harm the child. When analyzing interviews from her study, Donath notes significant verbal couching. The women in her study all regret having children; even then, the mothers recognize the complexity of their feelings. This "rhetorical maneuvering," Donath explains, underscores "the intensity of the social and cultural mechanisms" of motherhood, which are impossible to shake off "due to their institutionalization." Julie has been saying this to me for years. Women may air doubts privately, but social pressures dictate silence. And silence harms.

The poems from this little collection, *Happy Neighborhood*, come to grips with a simple truth: that being a parent is hard. I do not want to come off as sentimental. Through writing, I have tried settling into the happy neighborhood. I search for a contentment that does not come intuitively, a peace that needs to be cultivated or learned. The dog, starting with sunrise walks to the park, gave me a starting point; Virgil provided a structure and ritual for writing. The adoption of a child deepened my need to write. My family does not

gravitate to the positive. Julie checks every box on Konrad Piotrowski's taxonomy of parental regret. (When she is troubled, she
will unconsciously mumble, "Virgil.") The kid, now in his twenties
and living on his own, will have to make peace with his trauma. He
must come to a space of healing on his own time.

For me, for now, the poems help. Poetry has given me a space
to at least imagine a happy home. I write about tree forts and bike
ramps, chickens and heart pine trim; with draft after draft, I can strip
away the anger or resistance and, I hope, let natural beauty in. But
still…these lofty sentiments aside, I feel the stretch and strain of
afterthought.

I wonder especially if I have leaned too heavily upon the frame-
work of a house.

The myth of the happy home is its own shibboleth—a lie second only in magnitude to that of the virtuous, sacrificing parent.
Why do we cling to our beliefs about property? Stories, again, tell us
far more quantitative social studies. At the close of Arthur Miller's
Death of a Salesman, Willy Loman crashes his car to collect a life
insurance policy. The fraudulent accident culminates one of several
errors committed by the tragic anti-hero. His every misstep indicates
the unacknowledged regret at who he let himself become. Willy
cheats on his wife, lies to his sons, lies to himself, and kills himself
for no reason. He leaves this earth the shell of a man; only his closest
family attend his funeral. The inner delusions culminate with the
play's central irony, that Willy has died without knowing that he and
his wife Linda had paid off their mortgage. He cannot recognize his
own success.

How does Arthur Miller expose the fake dream being peddled
to our reading public? Is there a more chilling word in the English
language than *mortgage*? This term comes from the Old French,
"death pledge." With home ownership, Julie and I made the same
foolish pledge as Willy Loman. We bought into a structure of feeling that serves the banks—not us. Through the twentieth century,
US culture has fed all of us a myth that property ownership should
ground our emotional and financial well-being. The dream is so

deeply indoctrinated that we scarcely recognize the theft of our very lives. Banks structure payment plans over thirty-year spans, approving applications for people already in their sixties, while setting the principle at such a level that the loans are rarely paid in full.

Our collective behavior defies reason. We will freely take on a second "death pledge," borrowing against the equity of our first loan, to remodel a kitchen or expand a master suite—because our closets are too small, we want a back porch, or appliances have fallen out of fashion. Television programs, entire cable channels, support this cycle of renovation without remorse. Parents will not question that we need a kitchen island (with granite countertop) to properly raise our kids.

I do not mean to sound judgmental, like a shrill Thoreauvian.

In our own way, indeed, Julie and I have made a similar mistake. When I started the poems collected here, I wanted to believe our house was special. I needlessly cultivated a DIY aesthetic. I spent hours stripping the trim to the heart pine in the living room, agonizing over whether we should hang drywall over the original plaster, sinking native plants into a grass-free yard. As I pursued this hand-crafted look, shaving expenses, I ignored the mounting expenditure of time. What value does our property hold if I include every trip to the chain hardware store in our balance sheet? I wrote this cycle of poems about a family's home life, in the same way, sanding down each line with woefully inefficient revision. Now I am left wondering whether I too have been played.

Besides, I always knew the happy neighborhood would go up for sale someday. When Julie and I signed the death pledge, some twenty years ago, a certain type of person would have called the neighborhood "dicey" or "in transition." Deep down, we knew that property close to the water could only rise in value. As real estate in mid-sized (or "livable") cities has skyrocketed across the country, sure enough, our "happy neighborhood" has steadily appreciated. Anyone who sells at this point would miss the last bump or two— and so the once residential community is now for rent, with owners biding their time. Our neighbor across the street runs short-term vacation leases out of his garage apartment; I do not know most of the people on my own block, and most of our neighbors rent. Community bumps against the realities of the exchange.

That brings me to the present, with the poems here mostly complete. After the kid finished high school, Julie and I left the home for a swank downtown apartment. Julie did not want to go back. Cleaning overwhelms her emotionally. The house carries scars. The doors will not close on their jambs. Holes punched in the plaster unsettle me.

Barely a day passes when Julie and I do not think about selling our hippy house. Then we think again. The property is paid off. The kid is stable and living on his own but he still needs us here. So we keep it local. The native plants have set their roots. We have three citrus trees, all bearing fruit, and more wild coffee than I can give away; beautyberry and firebush draw butterflies off the front porch; a healthy row of Simpson's Stopper, with fluffy white flowers that mature into tiny coral berries, hides the ugly stockade fence by the concrete basketball court. We have built our lives around this place. We have filled our obligations. If those obligations feel too close, we can lock the doors to our house and leave. We can escape. A house need not define us. We can hop in our camper van and go.

Acknowledgments

The first reader of every word in this book was Julie Armstrong, and if the poems sometimes feel like little more than exercises in keeping a happy home, that is because they started off that way. My second biggest thank-you goes to Zackary Leroy Johnson Armstrong-Hallock, a loving son and now self-sufficient young man who continues to find his way in the world beautifully. The debt to my siblings and parents knows no bounds. Very skilled colleagues and friends have looked over parts (and the whole) of this manuscript over the past twenty years. Thanks to Joshua David Bellin, Joshua McKinney, Heather Jones, Anda Peterson, Gianmarc Manzione, M. L. Williams, Casey Blanton, Jessica Kester, Martha McKay Canter, Molly Sackler, and my thriving community of writers in St. Petersburg, Florida. Rick Campbell offered a number of key suggestions. A turning point came during a short residency at the Lillian E. Smith Center of Piedmont University, and a Georg Bollenbeck Fellowship at the University of Siegen (hosted by Marcel Hartwig) gave me time and space to review this manuscript as one unit.

Portions of *Happy Neighborhood* have appeared elsewhere, and to the editors of the following journals, again, I am deeply grateful: "Stripping a Cabinet," *Tampa Review*; "Tree Fort," *Journal of Florida Studies*; "Chicken Aubade," *ISLE: Interdisciplinary Studies in Literature and the Environment*; "Patriarchy Meets the Man-Eating Goddess," *womenwriters.net*; "Water Has Memory," *GeoHumanities*; "State of the State," *Glass Bottom Sky: 10 Years of Yellowjacket Press Poetry*, edited by Silvia Curbelo and Gregory Byrd. Lastly, I offer appreciation to Marc Jolley for encouraging me to keep writing poetry and eventually to submit my manuscript to Mercer University Press. My book has a good home. Please support our literary and academic journals, our small publishers, and university presses.

Notes

"Introduction: Tree Fort"
mezzo cammin
I own up to the silly pretention of quoting Dante, and the obvious first line of *The Inferno* at that, "Nel mezzo del cammin di nostra vita" (1:1). In addition to Henry Wadsworth Longfellow's "Mezzo Cammin," see also his comforting "The Day Is Done"— "Such songs have power to quiet / The restless pulse of care, / And come like the benediction / That follows after prayer," from Henry Wadsworth Longfellow, *Selected Poems*, edited by Lawrence Buell (New York: Penguin, 1988), 355.

And when I could
Anne Bradstreet, "Here Follows Some Verses upon the Burning of Our House July 10th, 1666. Copied Out of a Loose Paper," *Works*, edited by Jennine Hensley (Cambridge: Harvard University Press, 1967), 292.

I will abroad
George Herbert, "The Collar," *George Herbert and the Seventeenth-Century Religious Poets*, edited by Mario A. DiCesare (New York: Norton, 1978), 55.

Lassing Park
"In the evenings herons nest / in oak trees bending toward the west / and the moon and stars on their hallowed arc / keep their nightly watch over Lassing Park"; from Peter Meinke, "Lassing Park," from *Lassing Park and Other Poems*, with drawings by Jeanne Clark Meinke (Tampa: Yellowjacket Press, 2011), n.p.

"Square Grouper"
docks off Salt Creek

On Salt Creek as unofficial port of call for drug trafficking, see Jack Alexander, "Drug Raid Nabs 11," *St. Petersburg Evening Independent*, May 18, 1968, 3A. Accessed on "Friends of Salt Creek" timeline (https://friendsofsaltcreek.org).

right-wing contras
Allegations of the CIA supplying drugs for Nicaragua's "Contras" is a story that has swirled for decades between conspiracy theory and mainstream acceptance, with reporting by the *San Jose Mercury News'* Gary Webb challenged by mainstream media presses then (sadly after Webb committed suicide) reconsidered; Peter Kornbluh reviews the controversy in "Storm over 'Dark Alliance,'" *Columbia Journalism Review* (Jan./Feb. 1997).

no other pleasure
Cocaine, scientist Eric Nestler explains, causes a buildup of dopamine, yielding "enormously powerful feelings of pleasure," greater than thirst quenching or sex, so much that "some laboratory animals, if given a choice, will ignore food and keep taking cocaine until they starve"; see "The Neurobiology of Cocaine Addiction," *Addiction Science and Clinical Practice* 3, no. 1 (Dec. 2005): 4–10.

c-o-l-o-m-b-i-a
Playful, understandably frustrated Colombians market a t-shirt correcting the error, there's a hashtag for social media (#itscolombianotcolumbia), and even Barack Obama committed a rare diplomatic gaffe; Dan Molinski reports, "Colombians Are Tired of People Spelling Their Country's Name as 'Columbia,'" *The Wall Street Journal*, May 24, 2014.

"Interlude: Happy Neighborhood"
Poetry's purpose
See Ted Kooser, *The Poetry Home Repair Manual: Practical Advice for Beginning Poets* (Lincoln: University of Nebraska Press, 2005), xi.

Where all the time
St. Petersburg, *"The Sunshine City"* (St. Petersburg: The Record Company, 1922), n.p.

Florida Statutes
See chapter 743, "Domestic Relations," in the 2020 Florida Statutes (http://www.leg.state.fl.us).

allow others
Amal Treacher and Ilan Katz, "Narrative and Fantasy in Adoption," *Adoption & Fostering* 25, no. 3 (2001): 27–28.

fuck you up
Philip Larkin, "This Be the Verse," Poetry Foundation. The quip about childhood, originating from Flannery O'Connor but repeated endlessly on author websites and course syllabi, goes, "Anybody who has survived his childhood has enough information about life to last him the rest of his days"; see *Mystery and Manners: Occasional Prose* (New York: Macmillan, 1969), 84.

"Interlude: Stapler Poem (or Thanks for Nothing, Ezra Pound)"
epigraph
Sharon Olds, "The Language of the Brag," *Poetry Magazine*, http://poetrymagazines.org.uk).

any other choice
My university colleague V. Mark Durand writes that "[u]nless you believe your child has it within him- or herself to improve his or her behavior, you will ultimately fail in your efforts"; see *Optimistic Parenting: Hope and Help for Your Challenging Child* (Baltimore: Paul H. Brookes, 2011), 21.

longish dull/endure
Ezra Pound, *The ABC of Reading* (New York: New Directions, 1934), 13, 91.

old bitch
Ezra Pound, from "Hugh Selwyn Mauberley: E.P. Ode Pour L'Election de Son Sepulchre," *Selected Poems of Ezra Pound* (New York: New Directions, 1957), 64; T. S. Eliot, "The Love Song of J. Alfred Prufrock," *The Waste Land and Other Poems* (New York: Harcourt Brace Jovanovich, 1962), 4; William Carlos Williams, "This Is Just to Say," *Selected Poems*, edited by Charles Tomlinson (New York: New Directions, 1985), 74.

terms/bad critic
Ezra Pound, *The ABC of Reading*, 84.

poetry/poets
Ted Kooser, *The Poetry Home Repair Manual: Practical Advice for Beginning Poets*, 5.

"Shiners"
Exercise based on Peter Meinke's discussion of the pantoum, a form in which "the second and fourth lines" of a quatrain appear in the "first and third of the next"; see *The Shape of Poetry: A Practical Guide to Writing Poetry* (Tampa: University of Tampa Press, 1999), 97.

"Requisite Poem from the Point of View of a Kitchen Table"
Epigraph
Ezra Pound, *The ABC of Reading*, 62.

"My Mother Says"
refrain
The line "my mother says," prompted by the chapter "Imported Voices: Bringing Other Speakers into the Poem," and the appended

exercise, in Tony Hoagland with Kay Cosgrove, *The Art of Voice: Poetic Principles and Practice* (New York: Norton, 2019), 155.

"Interlude: Short Observation on Andrew Marvell"
As lines
Andrew Marvell, "The Definition of Love," *Complete Poems*, 49; Marvell riffs off John Donne's more famous "A Valediction: Forbidding Mourning," Poetry Foundation (https://www.poetryfoundation.org).

Low
In a letter to the "Forum" of *PMLA,* Anthony Low complains about the journal's revamped cover, and in response to the trending cultural (over literary) studies attempts sarcasm: "Surely anyone 'not receptive to cultural approaches'—or to whatever approaches are in vogue next month—should be exiled from the organization, dismissed from his or her job, and shot. That would instantly recuperate the signifying system by conjoining elements of historical, sociological, and anthropological insight in an expansive project of normative inclusiveness that would signal a danger only for the problematic exponents of a discredited, hegemonic, and (pseudo)academic remnant"; see "What Is Literature?" *PMLA* 110, no. 1 (Jan. 1995): 122–23.

dissociation
T. S. Eliot's phrase (then so famous as to not require citation) is quoted in Anthony Low, "Metaphysical Poets and Devotional Poets," *George Herbert and the Seventeenth-Century Religious Poets*, 222; I quote the core of Low's argument, "Metaphysical Poets and Devotional Poets," 223–25.

Eliot
"George Herbert as Religious Poet," excerpted in *George Herbert and the Seventeenth-Century Religious Poets*, 237–40.

Coleridge
"Letters," excerpted in *George Herbert and the Seventeenth-Century Religious Poets*, 232.

"Apologia, for my father"
I'm sorry
Exercise from Tony Hoagland with Kay Cosgrove, "write a poem of apology for something for which the speaker is in fact *not* sorry"; see *The Art of Voice: Poetic Principles and Practices*, 141.

"What We Pass Down, also for my father"
You killed
"Write a poem beginning with an apostrophe to someone special": Tony Hoagland with Kay Cosgrove, *The Art of Voice: Poetic Practices and Practice*, 126.

"On Hypotext, or how scripture got rewritten by the Chicago Seven"
hypotext
Hypotext, a term associated with the literary critic Gérard Genette, refers to the source text in a literary allusion, such as the *Odyssey* to Virgil's *Aeneid* or James Joyce's *Ulysses*; within hypotextual relations, Genette observes, the travesty "consists of transforming a noble text by imitating"; see *Palimpsests: Literature in the Second Degree*, trans. Channa Newman and Claude Doubinsky (Lincoln: University of Nebraska Press, 1997), 30.

Matthew 10:33-35
Hoffman quotes the book of Matthew in *The Trial of the Chicago 7*, dir. Aaron Sorkin (Los Gatos, CA: Netflix, 2020). Jeet Heer, in a discussion of how Sorkin softened the defendant's political edge, notes Hoffman's Yiddish taunts of his namesake Judge (also Hoffman) in "Aaron Sorkin Sanitizes the Chicago 7," *The Nation* (Oct. 21, 2020).

"On Some Problems Translating the Naufragios of Álvar Núñez Cabeza de Vaca"

This poem combines local (St. Petersburg) history with matters of language and theft inherent to colonialism. In 1528, the expedition led by Spanish conquistador Pánfilo de Narváez, which was chronicled by Álvar Núñez Cabeza de Vaca, landed somewhere off Tampa Bay, at which point the Requerimiento (the empty Spanish document, noting Native consent to the Spanish invasion) was read. "Windfucker," an obsolete term about one who manipulates language, is a favorite term of one of my writing mentors, Roy Peter Clark. The image of "cernicalo" is from Sebastián de Covarrubias Horozco, *Tesoro de la Lengua Castellana o Espaüola*, edited by Ignacio Arellano and Rafael Zafra (Pamplona, Spain: Universidad de Navarra Press, 2006); Covarrubias's aptly named *Tesoro* (1611) offers a treasury of language, incorporating both the aesthetic highs of the Spanish Golden Age and the infusion of verbal (and linguistic) wealth that followed the invasion of the Americas.

Panther

The Florida panther remains endangered due to consequences of habitat loss, or stolen land, with a study of collared cougars listing causes as "intraspecific aggression, infectious diseases, starvation, trauma from prey, vehicular trauma, research activities, drowning, electrocution, rattlesnake bite, atrial septal defects, aortic aneurysm, old age, and hunter harvest"; see Sharon K. Taylor, Claus D. Buergelt, Melody E. Roelke-Parker, Bruce L. Homer, and Dave S. Rotstein, "Causes of Mortality of Free Roaming Florida Panthers," *Journal of Wildlife Diseases* 38, no. 1 (2002): 107.

"Poetic Life in Dog Years (a pentimento)"
Pentimento
Jonathan Stephenson, "Pentiment," *Grove Art Online*.

Sargent

Dorothy Mahon and Silvia Centeno review the history of *Madame X* in "A Technical Study of John Singer Sargent's Portrait of Madame Pierre Gautreau," *Metropolitan Museum Journal* 40 (2005): 121–29. For comparison with the incriminating strap, see Sargent's *Madame X*, which can be accessed at the Metropolitan Museum of Art website (http://www.metmuseum.org).

Van Eyck

Rachel Billinge and Lorne Campbell, "The Infra-red Reflectograms of Jan van Eyck's Portrait of Giovanni(?) Arnolfini and his Wife Giovanna Cenani(?)," *National Gallery Technical Bulletin* 16 (1995): 47–60. The infrared images provide a fascinating glimpse into the painting's backstory. Note in particular the dog, a memorable later addition to the final piece (which is accessible at the National Gallery website), but that in the scholarly study appears to be a ghost in the carpet.

Swaby

Gio Swaby's "Fresh Up" was on show at St. Petersburg's Museum of Fine Arts May to October 2022 (https://mfastpete.org); for examples of the exposed thread, see her catalog, *Fresh Up* (New York: Rizzoli, 2022).

Interlude: Patriarchy Meets the Man-Eating Goddess
oposición
Gloria Anzaldúa, *Borderlands/La Frontera: The New Mestiza*, 2nd ed. (San Francisco: Aunt Lute Books, 1987), 51.

Spirit of Life

For the lyrics to this 1981 song, see Caroline McDade, "Spirit of Life," from the useful website *hymnary.org*.

"Florida Study"
dedication
Gary Mormino is my school's Frank E. Duckwall Professor of Florida History. He is the author of many books, beloved for his packets of photocopied newspaper clippings sent to friends far and wide, and the founding co-director of my school's Florida Studies Program. Mormino commonly signs his correspondence, "Florida Dreams."

"Hers"
bird tracks
Thomas Wentworth Higginson famously compared Emily Dickinson's handwriting to "fossil bird tracks" in "Emily Dickinson's Letters," *The Atlantic* (Oct. 1891).

Cincinnati
When writing this poem, I had it in my head that Lulu self-publishing was based out of Cincinnati, Ohio, but I was mistaken; it is a North Carolina company. An original, self-published prototype of *Happy Neighborhood* (one copy) was printed by Lulu for Julie Armstrong on Valentine's Day 2019.

"Water Has Memory"
Hydra Lacy
Hydra Lacy, formerly a St. Petersburg resident and brother of boxer Jeff Lacy, shot two police officers and was killed himself during a January 24, 2011, raid on the home of his wife Christine. *Boxing Insider* reported, "When attempts to remove Lacy from the attic failed and after Lacy shot two of the officers, who became trapped in the attic with Lacy, heavily armored tactical officers from across Tampa Bay rushed to the scene armed with small tanks equipped with battering rams to knock down doors and walls" (Jan. 25, 2011). The home was demolished without an investigation.

As all the Heavens were
a Bell,
And Being, but an Ear,
And I, and Silence, some
strange Race
Wrecked, solitary, here —

And then a Plank in
Reason, broke,
And I dropped down, and
down —
And hit a World, at every
+plunge,
And +Finished knowing — then —
Crash — +Got through —

Dickinson, "I felt a funeral."

limpkin

Naturalist Benjamin Smith Barton, following the lead of his Philadelphia friend (and Florida traveler) William Bartram, followed the Muscogean name in the first scientific report of the limpkin, "Some account of the Tantalus ephouskyca, a rare American Bird," *Transactions of the Linnean Society of London* 12 (1818): 24–27. To hear the cry of this bird (now *Aramas guarauna*), go to the "limpkin" page of the Cornell Ornithology lab site (www.allaboutbirds.org).

"Preparation"

Because

Irma S. Rombauer and Marion Rombauer Becker, "Buttermilk Biscuits," *Joy of Cooking* (Indianapolis: Bobbs-Merrill, 1931), 634.

Once upon

Rombauer and Rombauer Becker, *Joy of Cooking*, 599. This passage was revised in later editions: "In medieval England, the term for 'dough kneader' developed gradually into the word 'lady'—an indication of the justified respect, we have always thought, with which bread bakers have long been regarded"; see Irma S. Rombauer, Marion Rombauer Becker, and Ethan Becker, *Joy of Cooking* (New York: Scribner, 1997), 735.

Lady

from the *Compact Edition of the Oxford English Dictionary* (2:1558). The superscript to "loaf[1]" refers to the primary definition of that word, "portion of bread baked in one mass...."; the superscript in "dey[1]" refers to a "woman having charge of a dairy and things pertaining to it." The "<" (or "less than" arrow) signifies "from"; so "< loaf" means the word "lady" derives from the Old English word "loaf," "kneader" is from "*digan* to knead." But the asterisk used in an etymology, by the *OED*'s dense and delightfully arcane system of codes, "indicates a word or form not actually found but of which the existence is inferred" (2:xii). Meaning the etymology could be spurious? It deserves mention that the *OED* Victorian-era editorial staff included several women, which might explain the coded skepticism.

A reading of this passage is left to individual tastes. It would be up to individuals to decide whether to flesh out the annotations, skip them, read them simply as signs, or some combination of the three. I might suggest as follows: "Lady. Noun. Etymology [slight pause] from loaf, meaning the portion of bread baked in one mass, plus an otherwise unattested Old English, possibly though not entirely certain, from *dīge* [dijuh], or kneader, which compares to *dey*, noun, meaning a woman having charge of a dairy, from the same Germanic base as the Gothic *digan*, to knead."

This bread
Edward Taylor, *Poems*, edited by Donald E. Stanford (Chapel Hill: University of North Carolina Press, 1989), 18.

Does ripen
Wallace Stevens, *The Collected Poems* (New York: Vintage, 1982), 69.

"Lullaby"
Adaptation
The refrain quotes the film *Adaptation*, in which the lead character Charlie Kaufman (played by Nicholas Cage) reads from Susan Orlean's *The Orchid Thief: A True Story of Beauty and Obsession* (New York: Ballantine, 2000), 46–48.

"State of the State"
crook
Rick Scott, Governor of Florida when this poem was written, was CEO of the Columbia/HCA hospitals when the federal government fined the chain $1.7 billion for Medicare/Medicaid fraud and systematic overbilling; Andy Kroll, "The Rap Sheet on Rick Scott," this charge was repeated by Democratic opponents in later

political races, and while Scott was never directly convicted, he did head the company and the charge has been accepted as mostly true; see Amy Sherman, "Rick Scott oversaw 'the largest Medicare fraud in the nation's history'," *Politifact* (March 3, 2014).

"City House Poem, a close"
Zamia....
Latin plant names are also poetry; if possible, the reader may ask a partner to read the scientific nomenclature alongside the poem's body as a kind of interjection or running interruption.

"Camper Van"
three percent
Statistics on foster care children in college vary; bottom line, the percentage is low. I cite 3 percent from the webpage for National Foster Youth Institute, "Higher Education for Foster Youth" (https://nfyi.org/issues/higher-education/).

regret
On parental regret, see: Konrad Piotrowski, "How Many Parents Regret Having Children and How It Is Linked to Their Personality and Health: Two Studies with National Samples in Poland," *Plos One* (July 21, 2021); Orna Donath, "Regretting Motherhood: A Sociopolitical Analysis," *Signs* 40, no. 20 (Winter 2019): 360.

Miller
Adrienne Brown reviews the mythology of homeownership in a convincing essay, "1922–1968: The Disenchanted Literature of Homeownership," from *Timelines of American Literature*, edited by Cody Marrs and Christopher Hager (Baltimore: Johns Hopkins University Press, 2019), 37–52.

Mortgage

Definition from *The Compact Edition of the Oxford English Dictionary: Complete Text Reproduced Micrographically* (New York: Oxford University Press, 1971).

Bibliography

Alexander, Jack. "Drug Raid Nabs 11." *St. Petersburg Evening Independent*. May 18, 1968. 3A.

Alighieri, Dante. *The Divine Comedy: Inferno*. Translated by Allen Mandelbaum. New York: Bantam, 1982.

Anzaldúa, Gloria. *Borderlands/La Frontera: The New Mestiza*. San Francisco: Aunt Lute, 1987.

Barton, Benjamin Smith. "Some account of the Tantalus ephouskyca, a Rare American Bird." *Transactions of the Linnean Society of London* 12 (1818): 24–27.

Billinge, Rachel, and Lorne Campbell. "The Infra-red Reflectograms of Jan van Eyck's Portrait of Giovanni(?) Arnolfini and his Wife Giovanna Cenani(?)." *National Gallery Technical Bulletin* 16 (1995): 47–60.

Bradstreet, Anne. *Works*. Edited by Jeannine Hensley. Cambridge: Harvard University Press, 1967.

Brown, Adrienne. "1922–1968: The Disenchanted Literature of Homeownership." In *Timelines of American Literature*, edited by Cody Marrs and Christopher Hager, 37–52. Baltimore: Johns Hopkins University Press, 2019.

Cabeza de Vaca, Álvar Núñez de. *Chronicle of the Narváez Expedition*. Translated by Fanny Bandelier. New York: Penguin, 2002.

Covarrubias Horozco, Sebastián de. *Tesoro de la Lengua Castellana o Espaüola*. Edited by Ignacio Arellano and Rafael Zafra. Pamplona, Spain: Universidad de Navarra Press, 2006.

Dickinson, Emily. "I Felt a Funeral in My Brain." Emily Dickinson Archive, https://www.edickinson.org/editions/1/image_sets/401785.

Donath, Orna. "Regretting Motherhood: A Sociopolitical Analysis." *Signs* 40, no. 20 (Winter 2019): 343–67.

Donne, John. "A Valediction: Forbidding Mourning." Poetry Foundation, https://www.poetryfoundation.org/poems/44131/a-valediction-forbidding-mourning.

Durand, V. Mark. *Optimistic Parenting: Hope and Help for Your Challenging Child*. Baltimore: Paul H. Brookes, 2011.

Eliot, T. S. *The Waste Land and Other Poems*. New York: Harcourt Brace Jovanovich, 1962.

Florida Statutes (2020). "Domestic Relations: Disability of Nonage of Children Removed," http://www.leg.state.fl.us/statutes/index.cfm?App_mode=Display_Statute&URL=0700-0799/0743/Sections/0743.0645.html.

Genette, Gérard. *Palimpsests: Literature in the Second Degree*. Translated by Channa Newman and Claude Doubinsky. Lincoln: University of Nebraska Press, 1997.

Hallock, Thomas. *Happy Neighborhood (poems)*. St. Petersburg, FL: no publisher, 2019.

Heer, Jeet. "Aaron Sorkin Sanitizes the Chicago 7." *The Nation* (October 21, 2020), https://www.thenation.com/article/culture/chicago-7-trial-film/.

Herbert, George. *George Herbert and the Seventeenth-Century Religious Poets*. Edited by Mario A. DiCesare. New York: Norton, 1978.

Higginson, Thomas Wentworth. "Emily Dickinson's Letters." *The Atlantic* (October 1891), https://www.theatlantic.com/magazine/archive/1891/10/emily-dickinsons-letters/306524/.

Hoagland, Tony and Kay Cosgrove. *The Art of Voice: Poetic Principles and Practice*. New York: Norton, 2019.

"Jeff Lacy's Brother Causes Horrific Tragedy in St. Pete, Florida." *Boxing Insider* (January 25, 2011), https://www.boxinginsider.com/headlines/jeff-lacys-brother-causes-horrific-tragedy-in-st-pete-fl/.

Jonze, Spike, director. *Adaptation*. Columbia Pictures, Culver City, CA, 2002.

Kooser, Ted. *The Poetry Home Repair Manual: Practical Advice for Beginning Poets*. Lincoln: University of Nebraska Press, 2005.

Kornbluh, Peter. "Storm over 'Dark Alliance.'" *Columbia Journalism Review* (Jan./Feb. 1997), https://nsarchive2.gwu.edu/NSAEBB/-NSAEBB113/storm.htm.

Kroll, Andy. "The Rap Sheet on Rick Scott." *Mother Jones* (Nov. 2, 2010), https://www.motherjones.com/crime-justice/2010/11/rick-scott-alex-sink-florida/.

Larkin, Philip. "This Be the Verse." Poetry Foundation, https://www.poetryfoundation.org/poems/48419/this-be-the-verse.

"Limpkin." All About Birds (Cornell Ornithology Lab), https://www.allaboutbirds.org/guide/Limpkin/overview.

Longfellow, Henry Wadsworth. *Selected Poems*. Edited by Lawrence Buell. New York: Penguin, 1988.

Low, Anthony. "What Is Literature? ["Forum" letter]." *PMLA* 110, no. 1 (Jan. 1995): 122–23.

Mahon, Dorothy, and Silvia Centeno. "A Technical Study of John Singer Sargent's Portrait of Madame Pierre Gautreau." *Metropolitan Museum Journal* 40 (2005): 121–29.

Marvell, Andrew. *Complete Poems*. Edited by Elizabeth Story Donno. New York: Penguin, 1972.

McDade, Caroline. "Spirit of Life" (1981). *Hymnary*, https://hymnary.org/tune/spirit_of_life_mcdade.

Meinke, Peter. *Lassing Park*. Tampa: YellowJacket Press, 2011.

———. *The Shape of Poetry: A Practical Guide to Writing Poetry*. Tampa: University of Tampa Press, 1999.

Molinski, Dan. "Colombians Are Tired of People Spelling Their Country's Name as 'Columbia.'" *The Wall Street Journal* (May 24, 2014), https://www.wsj.com/articles/colombians-are-tired-of-people-misspelling-their-countrys-name-as-columbia-1398133196.

National Foster Youth Institute. "Higher Education for Foster Youth," https://nfyi.org/issues/higher-education/.

Nestler, Eric. "The Neurobiology of Cocaine Addiction." *Addiction Science and Clinical Practice* 3, no. 1 (December 2005): 4–10, https://www.ncbi.nlm.nih.gov/pmc/articles/PMC2851032/.

O'Connor, Flannery. *Mystery and Manners: Occasional Prose*. New York: Macmillan, 1969.

Olds, Sharon. "The Language of the Brag." *The North* 5 (1989). Reprinted in *Poetry Magazine*, http://poetrymagazines.org.uk/magazine/record08ba-2.html?id=2160.

Orlean, Susan. *The Orchid Thief: A True Story of Beauty and Obsession*. New York: Ballantine, 2000.

Oxford English Dictionary. Compact Edition. New York: Oxford University Press, 1971.

Piotrowski, Konrad. "How Many Parents Regret Having Children and How It Is Linked to Their Personality and Health: Two Studies with National Samples in Poland." *Plos One* (July 21, 2021), https://doi.org/10.1371/journal.pone.0254163

Pound, Ezra. *The ABC of Reading*. New York: New Directions, 1934.
———. *Selected Poems of Ezra Pound*. New York: New Directions, 1957.
Prince, Gerald. "Foreword," in *Palimpsests: Literature in the Second Degree*, by Gérard Genette. Lincoln: University of Nebraska Press, 1997.
Rombauer, Irma S., and Marion Rombauer Becker. *The Joy of Cooking*. Indianapolis: Bobbs-Merrill, 1931.
Rombauer, Irma S., Marion Rombauer Becker, and Ethan Becker. *The Joy of Cooking*. New York: Scribner, 1997.
Rothko, Mark. "The Rothko Chapel" (1971), http://www.rothkochapel.org/.
St. Petersburg, "The Sunshine City." St. Petersburg: The Record Company, 1922. Publication of Archival Library and Museum Materials: State University Library of Florida, http://palmm.digital.flvc.org/islandora/object/usf%3A68464#page/02/mode/1up.
Sargent, John Singer. *Madame X*. Metropolitan Museum of Art, https://www.metmuseum.org/art/collection/search/12127.
Sherman, Amy. "Rick Scott oversaw 'the largest medicaid fraud in U.S. history,' Florida Democratic Party Says." *Politifact* (March 3, 2014), https://www.politifact.com/factchecks/2014/mar/03/florida-democratic-party/rick-scott-rick-scott-oversaw-largest-medicare-fra/.
Sorkin, Aaron, director. *The Trial of the Chicago 7*. Netflix, Los Gatos, CA, 2020.
Stephenson, Jonathan. "Pentiment." *Grove Art Online* (2003), https://doi.org/10.1093/gao/9781884446054.article.T066222.
Stevens, Wallace. *The Collected Poems*. New York: Vintage, 1982.
Swaby, Gio. "Fresh Up." Museum of Fine Arts, St. Petersburg, https://mfastpete.org/exh/gio-swaby/.
———. *Fresh Up*. New York: Rizzoli, 2022.
Taylor, Edward. *Poems*. Edited by Donald E. Stanford. Chapel Hill: University of North Carolina Press, 1989.
Taylor, Sharon K., Claus D. Buergelt, Melody E. Roelke-Parker, Bruce L. Homer, and Dave S. Rotstein. "Causes of Mortality of Free Roaming Florida Panthers." *Journal of Wildlife Diseases* 38, no. 1 (2002): 107–14.
Treacher, Amal, and Ilan Katz. "Narrative and Fantasy in Adoption." *Adoption & Fostering* 25, no. 3 (2001): 20–28.

Van Eyck, Jan. "The Arnolfini Portrait." National Gallery (London), https://www.nationalgallery.org.uk/paintings/jan-van-eyck-the-arnolfini-portrait.

Williams, William Carlos. *Selected Poems*. Edited by Charles Tomlinson. New York: New Directions, 1985.

Images

St. Petersburg, the Sunshine City (St. Petersburg, FL: St. Petersburg Chamber of Commerce, 1922?). University of South Florida Libraries—Tampa Special Collections, University of South Florida, Tampa, FL. http://palmm.digital.flvc.org/islandora/object/usf%3A68464#page/02/mode/1up.

Bartram, William. "Hibiscus coccineus" (1767). Courtesy Knowsley Hall, Collections of the Earl of Derby.

Dickinson, Emily. "I Felt a Funeral" (from Fascicle 16). MS Am 1118.3 53c, Houghton Library, Harvard University. https://www.edickinson.org/editions/1/image_sets/12174464.

Ruysch, Hendrik. "Tinunculus Cenchis" (kestrel). *Theatrum universale omnium animalium, piscium, avium, quadrupedum, exanguium, aquaticorum, insectorum et angium: CCLX tabulis ornatum ex scriptoribus tam antiquis quam recentioribus Aristoteles, Theophrasto, Dioscoride… & aliis maxima curâ à J. Jonstonio collectum ac plus quam trecentis piscibus nuperrime ex Indiis Orientalibus allatis.* Amsterdam: R. & G. Wetstenios, 1718. https://hdl.handle.net/2027/ucm.5327383144.

Sargent, John Singer. Scrapbook photograph of John Singer Sargent, "Madame X" (ca. 1884), an earlier state of his portrait of Madame Pierre Gautreau. Courtesy Metropolitan Museum of Art.

Van Eyck, Jan. "Portrait of Giovanni (?) Arnolfini and his Wife Giovanna Cenami (?)," infrared reflogram mosaic. National Gallery (London).